2nd Workshop on Evaluating Vector-Space Representations for NLP (RepEval 2017)

AA007911

Copenhagen, Denmark
8 September 2017

ISBN: 978-1-5108-4750-7

Printed from e-media with permission by:

Curran Associates, Inc.
57 Morehouse Lane
Red Hook, NY 12571

Some format issues inherent in the e-media version may also appear in this print version.

Copyright© (2017) by the Association for Computational Linguistics
All rights reserved.

Printed by Curran Associates, Inc. (2017)

For permission requests, please contact the Association for Computational Linguistics at the address below.

Association for Computational Linguistics
209 N. Eighth Street
Stroudsburg, Pennsylvania 18360

Phone: 1-570-476-8006
Fax: 1-570-476-0860

acl@aclweb.org

Additional copies of this publication are available from:

Curran Associates, Inc.
57 Morehouse Lane
Red Hook, NY 12571 USA
Phone: 845-758-0400
Fax: 845-758-2633
Email: curran@proceedings.com
Web: www.proceedings.com

RepEval 2017

The 2nd Workshop on Evaluating Vector-Space Representations for NLP

Proceedings of the Workshop

September 8, 2017
Copenhagen, Denmark

©2017 The Association for Computational Linguistics

Introduction

This workshop deals with the evaluation of general-purpose vector representations for linguistic units (morphemes, words, phrases, sentences, etc). What distinguishes these representations (or embeddings) is that they are not trained with a specific application in mind, but rather to capture broadly useful features of the represented units. Another way to view their usage is through the lens of transfer learning: The embeddings are trained with one objective, but applied on others.

Evaluating general-purpose representation learning systems is fundamentally difficult. They can be trained on a variety of objectives, making simple intrinsic evaluations useless as a means of comparing methods. They are also meant to be applied to a variety of downstream tasks, which will place different demands on them, making no single extrinsic evaluation definitive. The best techniques for evaluating embedding methods in downstream tasks often require investing considerable time and resources in retraining large neural network models, making broad suites of downstream evaluations impractical. In many cases, especially for word-level embeddings, these constraints have led to the rise of dedicated evaluation tasks like similarity and analogy which are not directly related either to training objectives or to downstream tasks. Tasks like these can serve a valuable role in principle, but in practice performance on these tasks has not been highly predictive of downstream task performance.

This workshop aims foster discussion of these issues, and to support the search for high-quality general purpose representation learning techniques for NLP. The workshop will accept submissions through two tracks: a proposal track will showcase submitted proposals for new evaluation techniques, and a shared task will accept submissions of new general purpose sentence representation systems – for which standard evaluations are notably absent – which will be evaluated on a sentence understanding task.

Organizers:

Sam Bowman, New York University
Yoav Goldberg, Bar-Ilan University
Felix Hill, Google DeepMind
Angeliki Lazaridou, Google DeepMind
Omer Levy, University of Washington
Roi Reichart, Technion – Israel Institute of Technology
Anders Søgaard, University of Copenhagen

Program Committee:

Omri Abend
Mohit Bansal
Jose Camacho Collados
Billy Chiu
Allyson Ettinger
Sahar Ghannay
Anna Gladkova
Mohit Iyyer
Douwe Kiela
Arne Kohn
Andras Kornai
Farhana Liza
Oren Melamud
Dmitrijs Milajevs
Diarmuid O'Seaghdha
Marek Rei
Laura Rimell
Naomi Saphra
Roy Schwartz
Gabriel Stanovsky
Pontus Stenetorp
Karl Stratos
Yulia Tsvetkov
Ivan Vulic
Torsten Zesch

Invited Speaker:

Yejin Choi, University of Washington
Kyunghyun Cho, New York University
Jakob Uszkoreit, Google

Table of Contents

Conference Program

Friday, September 8, 2017

09:00–09:20 Opening Remarks

09:20–09:55 Shared task report

The RepEval 2017 Shared Task: Multi-Genre Natural Language Inference with Sentence Representations
Nikita Nangia, Adina Williams, Angeliki Lazaridou and Samuel Bowman

09:55–10:30 Yejin Choi (University of Washington)

10:30–11:00 Coffee Break (set up posters)

11:00–11:35 Jakob Uszkoreit (Google Research)

11:35–12:10 Kyunghyun Cho (New York University)

12:10–12:30 Few Minutes Madness (Evaluation Proposals)

Traversal-Free Word Vector Evaluation in Analogy Space
Xiaoyin Che, Nico Ring, Willi Raschkowski, Haojin Yang and Christoph Meinel

Hypothesis Testing based Intrinsic Evaluation of Word Embeddings
Nishant Gurnani

Evaluation of word embeddings against cognitive processes: primed reaction times in lexical decision and naming tasks
Jeremy Auguste, Arnaud Rey and Benoit Favre

Playing with Embeddings : Evaluating embeddings for Robot Language Learning through MUD Games
Anmol Gulati and Kumar Krishna Agrawal

Friday, September 8, 2017 (continued)

Recognizing Textual Entailment in Twitter Using Word Embeddings
Octavia-Maria Şulea

12:30–14:00 Lunch (somewhere together if pos)

14:00–14:30 Contributed Talks (shared task systems)

14:00–14:15 *Recurrent Neural Network-Based Sentence Encoder with Gated Attention for Natural Language Inference*
Qian Chen, Xiaodan Zhu, Zhen-Hua Ling, Si Wei, Hui Jiang and Diana Inkpen

14:15–14:30 *Shortcut-Stacked Sentence Encoders for Multi-Domain Inference*
Yixin Nie and Mohit Bansal

14:30–15:30 Posters and discussion

Character-level Intra Attention Network for Natural Language Inference
Han Yang, Marta R. Costa-jussà and José A. R. Fonollosa

Refining Raw Sentence Representations for Textual Entailment Recognition via Attention
Jorge Balazs, Edison Marrese-Taylor, Pablo Loyola and Yutaka Matsuo

LCT-MALTA's Submission to RepEval 2017 Shared Task
Hoa Vu

Friday, September 8, 2017 (continued)

15:30–16:00 Working Coffee Break

16:00–17:30 Presentation of Findings and Panel Discussion

16:00–17:30 *Presentation of Findings and Panel Discussion*
Yejin Choi, Kyunghyun Cho, Jakob Uszkoreit and other great minds if they are up for it...

The RepEval 2017 Shared Task: Multi-Genre Natural Language Inference with Sentence Representations

Nikita Nangia[1]
nikitanangia@nyu.edu

Adina Williams[2]
adinawilliams@nyu.edu

Angeliki Lazaridou[3]
angeliki@deepmind.com

Samuel R. Bowman[1,2]
bowman@nyu.edu

[1]Center for Data Science
New York University

[2]Department of Linguistics
New York University

[3]DeepMind

Abstract

This paper presents the results of the RepEval 2017 Shared Task, which evaluated neural network sentence representation learning models on the Multi-Genre Natural Language Inference corpus (MultiNLI) recently introduced by Williams et al. (2017). All of the five participating teams beat the bidirectional LSTM (BiLSTM) and continuous bag of words baselines reported in Williams et al.. The best single model used stacked BiLSTMs with residual connections to extract sentence features and reached 74.5% accuracy on the genre-matched test set. Surprisingly, the results of the competition were fairly consistent across the genre-matched and genre-mismatched test sets, and across subsets of the test data representing a variety of linguistic phenomena, suggesting that all of the submitted systems learned reasonably domain-independent representations for sentence meaning.

1 Introduction

The Second Workshop on Evaluating Vector Space Representations for NLP (RepEval 2017) features a shared task competition meant to evaluate natural language understanding models based on sentence encoders—that is, models that transform sentences into fixed-length vector representations and reason using those representations. Submitted systems are evaluated on the task of natural language inference (NLI, also known as recognizing textual entailment, or RTE) on the Multi-Genre NLI corpus (MultiNLI; Williams et al. 2017). Each example in the corpus consists of a pair of sentences, and systems must predict whether the relationship between the two sentences is *entailment*, *neutral* or *contradiction* in a balanced three-way classification setting.

We selected the task of NLI with the intent to evaluate as directly as possible the degree to which each model can extract and manipulate distributed representations of sentence meaning. In order for a system to perform well at natural language inference, it needs to handle nearly the full complexity of natural language understanding,[1] but its framing as a sentence-pair classification problem makes it suitable as an evaluation task for a broad range of models, and avoids issues of sequence generation, structured prediction, or memory access that can complicate evaluation in other settings.

The shared task includes two evaluations, a standard in-domain (*matched*) evaluation in which the training and test data are drawn from the same sources, and a cross-domain (*mismatched*) evaluation in which the training and test data differ substantially. This cross-domain evaluation tests the ability of submitted systems to learn representations of sentence meaning that capture broadly useful features.

This paper briefly introduces the task and dataset, presents the rules and results of the competition, and analyzes and compares the submitted systems. All the submitted systems are broadly

[1]Entailment notably does not require a system to ground its representations of sentence meaning to any outside representational system, for better or worse. For related discussion of entailment and natural language understanding see Chierchia and McConnell-Ginet (1991), Dagan et al. (2006), and MacCartney (2009).

Proceedings of the 2nd Workshop on Evaluating Vector-Space Representations for NLP, pages 1–10,
Copenhagen, Denmark, September 7–11, 2017. ©2017 Association for Computational Linguistics

Premise	Genre / Label	Hypothesis
Met my first girlfriend that way.	FACE-TO-FACE **contradiction**	I didn't meet my first girlfriend until later.
He turned and saw Jon sleeping in his half-tent.	FICTION **entailment**	He saw Jon was asleep.
8 million in relief in the form of emergency housing.	GOVERNMENT **neutral**	The 8 million dollars for emergency housing was still not enough to solve the problem.
Now, as children tend their gardens, they have a new appreciation of their relationship to the land, their cultural heritage, and their community.	LETTERS **neutral**	All of the children love working in their gardens.
At 8:34, the Boston Center controller received a third transmission from American 11	9/11 **entailment**	The Boston Center controller got a third transmission from American 11.
In contrast, suppliers that have continued to innovate and expand their use of the four practices, as well as other activities described in previous chapters, keep outperforming the industry as a whole.	OUP **contradiction**	The suppliers that continued to innovate in their use of the four practices consistently underperformed in the industry.
I am a lacto-vegetarian.	SLATE **neutral**	I enjoy eating cheese too much to abstain from dairy.
someone else noticed it and i said well i guess that's true and it was somewhat melodious in other words it wasn't just you know it was really funny	TELEPHONE **contradiction**	No one noticed and it wasn't funny at all.
For more than 26 centuries it has witnessed countless declines, falls, and rebirths, and today continues to resist the assaults of brutal modernity in its time-locked, color-rich historical center.	TRAVEL **entailment**	It has been around for more than 26 centuries.
If you need this book, it is probably too late' unless you are about to take an SAT or GRE.	VERBATIM **contradiction**	It's never too late, unless you're about to take a test.

Table 1: Randomly chosen examples from each genre of the MultiNLI development set.

similar, and incorporate bidirectional recurrent neural networks as a key component. We find that all systems performed fairly well, outperforming a simple bidirectional LSTM (BiLSTM; Hochreiter and Schmidhuber, 1997) baseline. To our surprise, no system performed dramatically worse on the *mismatched* evaluation than on the *matched* evaluation, and all systems performed reasonably consistently across examples representing a range of linguistic phenomena, suggesting that all were able to produce systems for semantic representation which, while not perfect, were effective and not tightly adapted to any particular style of language or set of constructions.

2 Dataset

MultiNLI (Williams et al., 2017) consists of 393k pairs of sentences from a broad range of genres of written and spoken English, balanced across three labels. Each premise sentence (the first sentence in each pair) is derived from one of ten sources of text, which constitute the ten genre sections of the corpus. Each hypothesis sentence and pair label was composed by a crowd worker in response to a premise. MultiNLI was designed and collected in the style of the Stanford NLI Corpus (SNLI; Bowman et al. 2015), but covers a broader range of styles of text, rather than the relatively homogeneous captions used in SNLI.

Testing and development sets are available for all genres, with 2000 examples per set per genre. Only five genres have accompanying training sets. So, for the *matched* development and test sets, models are tested on examples derived from the same sources as those in the training set, while for the *mismatched* sets, the text source is not represented in the training data.

Table 1 presents example sentences from the corpus and Table 2 presents some key statistics. For a detailed discussion of the corpus, refer to Williams et al. (2017).

3 Shared Task Competition

The purpose of the shard task is to evaluate techniques for training and using sentence encoders. To this end, we require that all models create fixed-length vectors for each sentence with no explicitly-imposed internal structure. Alignment strategies like attention that pass information between the two encoders handling the two input sentences in a pair are not allowed. Memory models that represent sentences as variable-length sets or sequences of vectors are also not permitted. While systems that use methods like attention and structured memory are effective for NLI (Rocktäschel et al., 2016; Wang and Jiang, 2016; Chen et al., 2017a; Williams et al., 2017, i.a.), much of the variation across models of this kind lies in the way that they explicitly or implicitly align related sentences, rather than the way that they extract representations for sentences. As a result, we expect that focusing our evaluation on a restricted subset of models will yield conclusions that are more generally applicable to work on natural language understanding than would have been the case otherwise.

Additional Rules We provide competitors with labeled training and development sets, and unlabeled test sets for which they must submit labels. The development sets are meant to be used for hyperparameter tuning and model selection, and training on the development sets is not allowed. We place no limits on the use of outside training data and resources except that they be publicly available. We specifically encourage the use of the SNLI training set. Multiple submissions from the same team are allowed, up to a limit of two per day during the two-week evaluation period. Individual participants (i.e., PIs) are permitted to join multiple teams within reason, but only when each team reflects a fully independent engineering effort and each team has a different lead developer.

Evaluation Competitors had approximately ten weeks, starting with the release of the MultiNLI training and development sets, to develop their systems and two additional weeks—the evaluation period—to run their systems on the unlabeled test sets and submit results. The shared task evaluation was hosted through the Kaggle in Class platform using two competition pages—one each for the *matched*[2] and *mismatched*[3] sections of the corpus. The public leaderboard, which was displayed during the evaluation period, showed results on a random 25% of the test set labels, and the final results were computed by evaluating the two best systems from each competitor (chosen from the public leaderboard) on the remaining hidden 75% of the test set labels.

4 Results and Leaderboard

The competition results are shown in Table 3. All evaluated systems beat the BiLSTM baseline reported in Williams et al.. Furthermore, there is only a marginal gap between accuracy on *matched* and *mismatched* test sets for all systems.

The best performing single model is by Nie and Bansal, who achieve the best result on the *matched* competition and tie with Chen et al. in the *mismatched* competition. The Nie and Bansal model architecture uses stacked BiLSTMs with residual connections and, unlike the other high performing models, does not use within-sentence attention. The best performing system overall is an ensemble by Chen et al., which is based closely on the Enhanced Sequential Inference Model (ESIM; Chen et al., 2017a) but with attention only within each sentence, rather than between the two.

Looking toward the future, we also made available non-time-limited Kaggle in Class competition pages[4] to allow for further fair evaluations on the MultiNLI test sets. Note that since these evaluation sites report results on 100% of the test set, rather than the 75% used in the shared task, numbers reported on that site may differ slightly from those seen in the competition.

5 Model Comparison

All of the submitted systems are based on bidirectional LSTMs, but each system uses this core tool in a somewhat different way. This section sur-

[2]`https://inclass.kaggle.com/c/multinli-matched-evaluation`

[3]`https://inclass.kaggle.com/c/multinli-mismatched-evaluation`

[4]Matched: `https://inclass.kaggle.com/c/multinli-matched-open-evaluation`
Mismatched: `https://inclass.kaggle.com/c/multinli-mismatched-open-evaluation`

Genre	#Examples Train	Dev.	Test	#Wds. Prem.	'S' parses Prem.	Hyp.	Agrmt.	BiLSTM Acc.
SNLI	*550,152*	*10,000*	*10,000*	*14.1*	*74%*	*88%*	*89.0%*	*81.5%*
FICTION	77,348	2,000	2,000	14.4	94%	97%	89.4%	66.8%
GOVERNMENT	77,350	2,000	2,000	24.4	90%	97%	87.4%	68.0%
SLATE	77,306	2,000	2,000	21.4	94%	98%	87.1%	68.4%
TELEPHONE	83,348	2,000	2,000	25.9	71%	97%	88.3%	67.7%
TRAVEL	77,350	2,000	2,000	24.9	97%	98%	89.9%	66.8%
9/11	0	2,000	2,000	20.6	98%	99%	90.1%	68.5%
FACE-TO-FACE	0	2,000	2,000	18.1	91%	96%	89.5%	67.5%
LETTERS	0	2,000	2,000	20.0	95%	98%	90.1%	66.4%
OUP	0	2,000	2,000	25.7	96%	98%	88.1%	66.7%
VERBATIM	0	2,000	2,000	28.3	93%	97%	87.3%	67.2%
MultiNLI Overall	**392,702**	**20,000**	**20,000**	**22.3**	**91%**	**98%**	**88.7%**	**67.4%**

Table 2: Key statistics for the corpus broken down by genre, presented alongside figures from SNLI for comparison. The first five genres represent the *matched* section of the development and test sets, and the remaining five represent the *mismatched* section. The first three statistics shown are the number of examples in each genre. *#Wds. Prem.* is the mean token count among premise sentences. *'S' parses* is the percentage of premises or hypotheses which the Stanford Parser labeled as full sentences rather than fragments. *Agrmt.* is the percent of individual annotator labels that match the assigned gold label used in evaluation. *BiLSTM Acc.* gives the test accuracy on the full test set for the BiLSTM baseline model trained on MultiNLI and SNLI.

Team Name	Authors	Matched	Mismatched	Model Details
alpha (ensemble)	Chen et al.	**74.9%**	**74.9%**	STACK, CHAR, ATTN., POOL, PRODDIFF
YixinNie-UNC-NLP	Nie and Bansal	74.5%	73.5%	STACK, POOL, PRODDIFF, SNLI
alpha	Chen et al.	73.5%	73.6%	STACK, CHAR, ATTN, POOL, PRODDIFF
Rivercorners (ensemble)	Balazs et al.	72.2%	72.8%	ATTN, POOL, PRODDIFF, SNLI
Rivercorners	Balazs et al.	72.1%	72.1%	ATTN, POOL, PRODDIFF, SNLI
LCT-MALTA	Vu et al.	70.7%	70.8%	CHAR, ENHEMB, PRODDIFF, POOL
TALP-UPC	Yang et al.	67.9%	68.2%	CHAR, ATTN, SNLI
BiLSTM baseline	Williams et al.	67.0%	67.6%	POOL, PRODDIFF, SNLI

Table 3: RepEval 2017 shared task competition results. The Model Details column lists some of the key strategies used in each system, using keywords: STACK: use of multilayer bidirectional RNNs, CHAR: character-level embeddings, ENHEMB: embeddings enhanced with auxiliary features, POOL: max or mean pooling over RNN states, ATTN: intra-sentence attention, PRODDIFF: elementwise sentence product and difference features in the final entailment classifier, SNLI: use of the SNLI training set.

veys the key differences between systems, and the Model Details column in Table 3 serves as a summary reference for these differences.

Depth Chen et al. and Nie and Bansal use three-layer bidirectional RNNs, while others only used single-layer RNNs. This likely contributes significantly to their good performance, as it is the most prominent feature shared only by these two top systems. They both use shortcut connections between recurrent layers to ease gradient flow, and Nie and Bansal find in an ablation study that using shortcut connections improves their performance by over 1% on both development sets.

Embeddings Systems vary reasonably widely in their approach to input encoding. Yang et al. and Chen et al. use a combination of GloVe embeddings (Pennington et al., 2014, not fine tuned) and character-level convolutional neural networks (Kim et al., 2016) to extract representations of words. Balazs et al. also use pre-trained GloVe embeddings without fine tuning, but report (contra Chen et al.) that an added character-level feature extractor does not improve performance.

Vu et al. use pre-trained GloVe word embeddings augmented with additional feature vectors. They create embeddings for part-of-speech (POS), character level information, and the dependency relation between a word and its parent, and concatenate these with the embedding for each word. They find that this supplies a small but nontrivial improvement to their development set performance, especially in the *mismatched* setting.

Nie and Bansal use the simplest strategy, initializing embeddings with GloVe vectors and fine-tuning them.

Pooling Vu et al. make a surprisingly effective change to the baseline BiLSTM model, motivated by Conneau et al.'s (2017) findings, by using max pooling rather than mean pooling when collecting the hidden states of the bidirectional LSTM for use as a sentence representation. They find that this yields an improvement of over 2.5% on both development sets.

While Vu et al. show that the choice of pooling strategy is quite important, Balazs et al. do not find a substantial effect in a similar comparison. This may be because Balazs et al.'s model also makes use of intra-sentence attention following the pooling layer, which dramatically reduces the importance of pooling.

Intra-Sentence Attention Chen et al. and Balazs et al. both use attention over the BiLSTM states of each sentence to compute a final representation for that sentence. Chen et al. in particular uses a novel *gated* attention formulation, in which the BiLSTM gate values supply the attention weights over hidden states according to

$$v_g = \sum_{i=1}^{n} \frac{\|g_i\|_2}{\sum_{j=1}^{n} \|g_j\|_2} h_i$$

where g_i is the BiLSTM input gate and h_i is the output from the BiLSTM encoder. They find that their use of gated attention helps performance somewhat relative to an unspecified baseline, though only in the *matched* setting.

Sentence Pair Classifier Every system but Yang et al.'s uses elementwise product and difference features, comparing the two sentence encodings as part of the input to the classifier MLP that predicts the final relation label. In an ablation study, Chen et al. find this to be highly important, yielding more than a 3% gain in performance on both development sets.

Data and SNLI We observe relatively little variation in the training data used in submitted systems. All systems are trained only on labeled NLI data—either the MultiNLI training set alone, or the MultiNLI and SNLI training sets combined. While Williams et al. find that the combined training set yields somewhat better results on the MultiNLI test set, Chen et al. nonetheless reaches state-of-the-art performance without using it.

Interim Discussion We were particularly struck by the effectiveness of the max pooling strategy as a simple and highly effective improvement to the baseline BiLSTM sentence encoder. Less surprisingly, depth and intra-sentence attention appear to be broadly effective, and product and difference features appear to be valuable when using sentence encoders for the task of NLI. The results surrounding embeddings and input encoding were less clear, though Nie and Bansal's use of pre-trained GloVe embeddings with fine tuning appears to be a simple and effective approach.

6 Error Analysis

In the interest of better understanding both the corpus and the submitted models, we annotate a 1,000-sample subset of the development set. We also provide a set of probe sentences and ask participating teams to submit vectors for all sentences in the probe set and test set. This section surveys our methods findings.

6.1 Annotations

The annotated subset of the development set was released to competitors during the model development period, and consists of 1,000 examples each tagged with zero or more of the following labels. Labels were assigned manually except where clear keyword-spotting techniques sufficed.

- CONDITIONAL: Whether either sentence contains a conditional.
  Example: **P:** *Laser-cutting equipment must be totally enclosed to be safe for human operators.* **H:** *Even if the laser machine is fully contained within, there still exist some amount of risk for the workers in the close proximity.*

- ACTIVE/PASSIVE: Whether there is an active-to-passive (or vice versa) transformation from the premise to the hypothesis.
  Example: **P:** *Hani Hanjour, Khalid Al Mihdhar, and Majed Moqed were flagged by capps.* **H:** *Capps never flagged anyone.*

	Annotation Tag	Label Frequency	BiLSTM	Yang	Balazs (S)	Chen (S)
Matched	CONDITIONAL	5%	100%	100%	100%	100%
	WORD_OVERLAP	6%	50%	63%	63%	63%
	NEGATION	26%	71%	75%	75%	75%
	ANTO	3%	67%	50%	50%	50%
	LONG_SENTENCE	20%	50%	**75%**	**75%**	67%
	TENSE_DIFFERENCE	10%	64%	68%	68%	**86%**
	ACTIVE/PASSIVE	3%	75%	75%	75%	88%
	PARAPHRASE	5%	78%	83%	83%	78%
	QUANTITY/TIME_REASONING	3%	50%	50%	50%	33%
	COREF	6%	83%	83%	83%	83%
	QUANTIFIER	25%	64%	59%	59%	**74%**
	MODAL	29%	66%	65%	65%	**75%**
	BELIEF	13%	74%	71%	71%	73%
Mismatched	CONDITIONAL	5%	100%	80%	80%	100%
	WORD_OVERLAP	7%	58%	62%	62%	76%
	NEGATION	21%	69%	73%	73%	72%
	ANTO	4%	58%	58%	58%	58%
	LONG_SENTENCE	20%	55%	67%	67%	67%
	TENSE_DIFFERENCE	4%	71%	71%	71%	89%
	ACTIVE/PASSIVE	2%	82%	82%	82%	91%
	PARAPHRASE	7%	81%	89%	89%	89%
	QUANTITY/TIME_REASONING	8%	46%	54%	54%	46%
	COREF	6%	80%	70%	70%	80%
	QUANTIFIER	28%	70%	68%	68%	**77%**
	MODAL	25%	67%	67%	67%	**76%**
	BELIEF	12%	73%	71%	71%	74%

Table 4: This table shows the accuracy of different models for each tagged subset of our 1,000-example development set sample. The '(S)' indicates that results for the single model are shown. Some results that stand out to us are shown in bold.

- PARAPHRASE: Whether the two sentences are close paraphrases.
  Example: **P:** *Uh, lets see.* **H:** *Let us look.*

- COREF: Whether the hypothesis contains a pronoun or referring expression that needs to be resolved using the premise.
  Example: **P:** *You and I, gentle reader, are accredited members of the guild.* **H:** *We are recognised as members of the guild.*

- QUANTIFIER: Whether either sentence contains one of the following quantifiers: *much, enough, more, most, less, least, no, none, some, any, many, few, several, almost, nearly.*
  Example: **P:** *We have provided an invoice to facilitate your gift.* **H:** *There's no invoice available for your gift.*

- MODAL: Whether either sentence contains one of the following modal verbs: *can, could, may, might, must, will, would, should.*
  Example: **P:** *Conversely, an increase in government saving adds to the supply of resources available for investment and may put downward pressure on interest rates.* **H:** *The amount of resources available for investment increases when government savings are increased.*

- BELIEF: Whether either sentence contains one of the following belief verbs: *know, believe, understand, doubt, think, suppose, recognize, recognize, forget, remember, imagine, mean, agree, disagree, deny, promise.*
  Example: **P:** *I trust that this is a fillip of propaganda and not a serious query.* **H:** *I believe this is to get attention and not a real inquiry.*

- NEGATION: Whether either sentence contains negation.
  Example: **P:** *On reflection, the parts will hold together.* **H:** *The parts will not hold together.*

- ANTO: Whether the two sentences contain an antonym pair.
  Example: **P:** *As united 93 left Newark, the flight's crew members were unaware of the hijacking of American 11.* **H:** *As the flight United 93 left Newark the crew members were fully aware of the hijacking of American 11.*

- TENSE_DIFFERENCE: Whether the two sentences use different tenses on any verbs.
  Example: **P:** *Does she like what she does?* **H:** *Does she like what she is doing?*

- QUANTITY/TIME_REASONING: Whether understanding the pair requires quantity or time reasoning.
  Example: **P:** *The vice chairman joined the conference shortly before 10:00; the secretary, shortly before 10:30.* **H:** *The secretary joined before the vice chairman.*

- WORD_OVERLAP: Whether the two sentences share more than 70% of their tokens.
  Example: **P:** *Let's look for paua shells!* **H:** *Let's look for sticks.*

- LONG_SENTENCE: Whether the premise or hypothesis is longer than 30 or 16 words respectively.
  Example: **P:** *As invested with its dignity, since the seventeenth century just as the crown has been used for the monarch, or the oval office has come to stand for the president of the United States.* **H:** *Nobody in Britain associates the crown with the monarchy.*

Table 4 shows model results on tagged examples for the BiLSTM baseline and for the three systems for which we were able to acquire example-by-example development set results (submission of these results was optional). Among those tags that are frequent enough to yield clearly interpretable numbers, none indicates a subset of the corpus that is dramatically harder or easier for the submitted models than is the corpus overall. This suggests that—as is typical with neural network models—these models do not rely strongly on any particular structural properties of the input texts to the exclusion of others.

We note that the submitted systems that use intra-attention (the three shown) do relatively well on the LONG_SENTENCE and NEGATION tags. This technique likely helps the encoders to recover the structures of long sentences and to correctly identify the scope of instances of negation. We also note that all systems do relatively poorly on the QUANTITY/TIME_REASONING section, suggesting that these simple sentence feature extractors are not well situated to learn quantitative reasoning in this setting.

Authors	1-NN Genre Accuracy
Chen et al.	67.3%
Nie and Bansal	74.0%
Balazs et al.	69.2%
Vu et al.	67.0%
Yang et al.	54.7%

Table 5: A thousand sentences are randomly sampled from the *matched* test set and their pairwise distances to all sentences in the test set (premises and hypotheses) are calculated. This table shows the percentage of times the first nearest neighbor belongs to the same genre as the sample sentence.

6.2 Nearest Neighbors

Test Set Sentences The competition participants were asked to submit sentence vectors for all the premise and hypothesis sentences in the test sets. We randomly sample 1,000 sentences from the *matched* test set and, using cosine similarity, calculate their pairwise distances against all sentences in the *matched* test set. Table 5 shows the percentage of times the first nearest neighbor belongs to the same genre as the chosen sentence. All models score fairly highly on this metric, suggesting that the learned representations are not genre-agnostic, despite their effectiveness in unseen genres. The models with higher percentage accuracy on the NLI task (see Table 3) show better performance on this metric as well, suggesting that this genre clustering property correlates with the overall quality of the metric space that each model uses to represent sentences.

The better models are also more interpretable. Table 6 shows example sentences and their three nearest neighbors for all models. It appears that entity identity is important for the Nie and Bansal model, though not it a way that is tied to syntactic position. For the *Critics loved Merchant-Ivory* example, we see matches to critics. In the *Students love the rich culture* example, we similarly see many matches to school and love. Since for each premise sentence in the MultiNLI corpus, there are 3 associated hypothesis sentences, it's not surprising to see that the first nearest neighbor is often one of these associated sentences, like in the *Critics* example where the first nearest neighbor for all systems is the premise sentence. We found that for some examples, the better performing systems like Nie and Bansal's had all three as-

Sample	Model	Nearest Neighbours	
Students love the rich culture and history of the school. (TR.)	Chen	TEL.	my son loved learning about computers in high school
		TR.	Families love this city-within-a-city on the beach.
		TR.	The urban working class loved the new factories.
	Nie	TEL.	my son loved learning about computers in high school
		TEL.	I really loved it when I was in middle school.
		SL.	A librarian and fellow patient kindled his love for literature more than school.
	Balazs	SL.	School, more than anything else, was credited for his love of literature.
		SL.	A librarian and fellow patient kindled his love for literature more than school.
		TEL.	I really loved it when I was in middle school.
	Vu	SL.	A librarian and fellow patient kindled his love for literature more than school.
		TR.	France's oldest city is a wonderful destination, with rich history and extreme beauty.
		FIC.	The rave had some of the best artists and celebrities.
	Yang	TR.	The urban working class loved the new factories.
		FIC.	my son loved learning about computers in high school
		TR.	This area is a favorite of hikers who enjoy invigorating journeys through dense forests and along the river valleys celebrated in the paintings of Gustave Courbet.
Critics loved Merchant-Ivory's final movie, which was an adaption of a novel written by Kaylie Jones. (SL.)	Chen	SL.	Critics laud Merchant-Ivory's exit from the 19th century in this adaptation of a semiautobiographical novel by Kaylie Jones (daughter of novelist James Jones).
		SL.	I loved Begnigni's movie!
		SL.	Mercer was the lifelong love of Franklin Roosevelt, and the revelation of their affair nearly ended his marriage to Eleanor.
	Nie	SL.	Critics laud Merchant-Ivory's exit from the 19th century in this adaptation of a semiautobiographical novel by Kaylie Jones (daughter of novelist James Jones).
		SL.	Critics find the book entertaining, praising digressions on gambling, laughing, and love, as well as Pinker's pop-culture references.
		SL.	Critics think that Lichtenstein was a contemporary genius.
	Balazs	SL.	Critics laud Merchant-Ivory's exit from the 19th century in this adaptation of a semiautobiographical novel by Kaylie Jones (daughter of novelist James Jones).
		TEL.	The period of the civil war is very interesting to me, I've read about 3 novels about that, including John Jakes ones.
		SL.	The most vivid moments in Kubrick's films in the last 30 years have come when he has turned his actor's faces into Think of Malcolm McDowell in A Clockwork Orange (1971), Jack Nicholson in The Shining (1980), and Vincent D'Onofrio in Full Metal Jacket (1987).
	Vu	SL.	Critics laud Merchant-Ivory's exit from the 19th century in this adaptation of a semiautobiographical novel by Kaylie Jones (daughter of novelist James Jones).
		SL.	Mercer was the lifelong love of Franklin Roosevelt, and the revelation of their affair nearly ended his marriage to Eleanor.
		SL.	Critics find the book entertaining, praising digressions on gambling, laughing, and love, as well as Pinker's pop-culture references.
	Yang	SL.	Critics laud Merchant-Ivory's exit from the 19th century in this adaptation of a semiautobiographical novel by Kaylie Jones (daughter of novelist James Jones).
		TR.	Visitors are encouraged to come during daylight hours, when the park is safer and better patrolled by employees.
		TR.	All Ireland loves a horse, and County Kildare can claim to be at the heart of horse country.

Table 6: Showing the three nearest neighbors for example sentences from a random 1,000-sample subset of the *matched* test set. All results are for single (non-ensemble) models. The genres have been abbreviated.

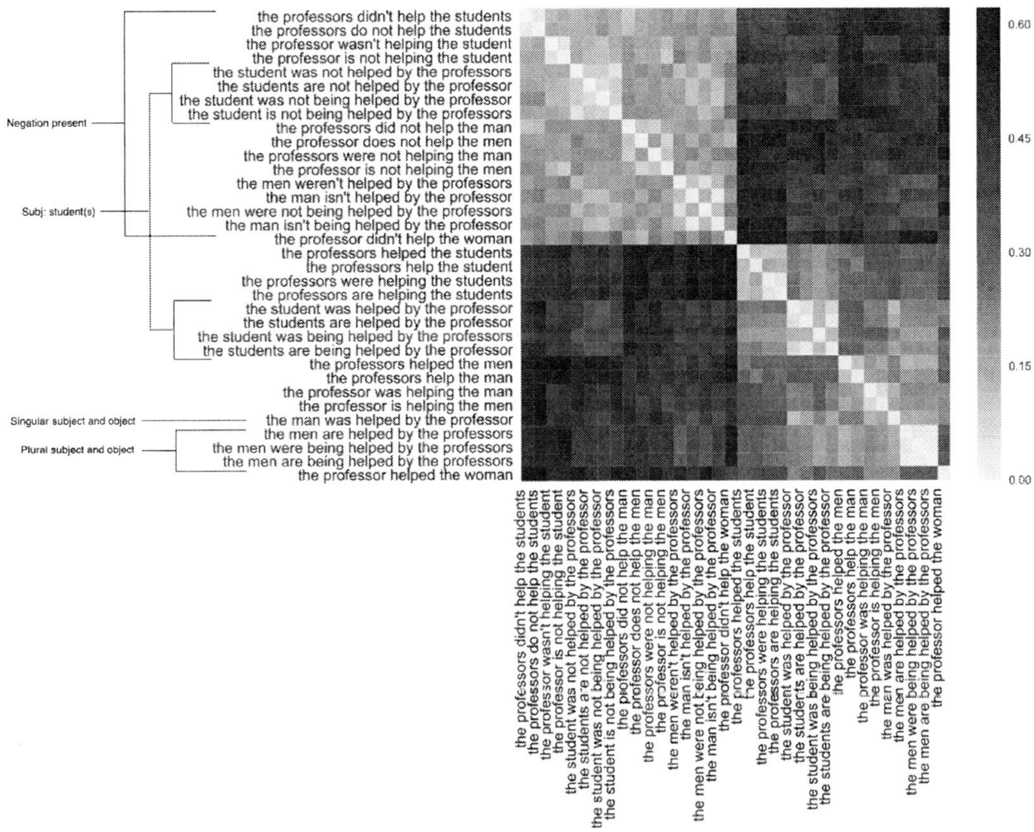

Figure 1: A heatmap showing the cosine similarity between sentence vectors. The vectors were rendered by the Nie and Bansal model. The plots for other systems are very similar.

sociated sentences as their top three nearest neighbors.

Probe Sentences During the competition, we additionally provided a set of automatically generated probe sentences meant to aid error analysis. These probe sentences are produced to vary along dimensions relevant to probing for semantic role and negation information. We asked submitting teams to supply vectors for these sentences in addition to those in the test set. Figure 1 shows the cosine similarity between a subset of these sentence vectors rendered by Nie and Bansal's (2017) system. We find that all systems (except that of Balazs et al., who did not submit these vectors) show similar behavior on these sentences, and we do not observe a clear correlation between behavior here and model performance. Perhaps unsurprisingly, we observe that sentences tend to be more similar to one another the more structural features they have in common. We observe this clearly for negation, identity of the subject, and tense, though continuous tenses are not reliably differentiated from others.

7 Conclusion

We find that BiLSTM-based models with max pooling or intra-sentence attention represent a popular and effective strategy for sentence encoding, and that systems based on this technique perform very well at the task of NLI.

We note that all submitted systems performed reasonably well across the many subsets of the data reflected by our supplementary tags, suggesting that none of these models exploit any particular narrow feature of the task or data to perform well. We also note that model performance does not vary much between the *matched* and *mismatched* sections of the test set. This means that submitted systems are likely capturing reasonably general strategies for extracting representations of meaning from text. As the systems get better, and fit the training data more closely, the disparity between *matched* and *mismatched* sets may appear. Both of these findings, though, bolster our expectation that the best of the submitted systems represent some of the best general-purpose architectures for sentence encoding available.

However, the task of NLI is far from being solved, and no submitted system approaches human performance, suggesting that there is ample room for further research on both the task and on the more general problem of sentence representation learning. Since many of the examples in MultiNLI require substantial commonsense background knowledge to solve fully, we suspect that the use of large outside datasets and resources (labeled or otherwise) will be crucial to making substantial further progress in this setting.

Acknowledgments

This work was made possible by a Google Faculty Research Award to Sam Bowman and Angeliki Lazaridou, and was also supported by a gift from Tencent Holdings. Allyson Ettinger contributed the supplementary probe sentences. We also thank George Dahl and the organizers of the RepEval 2016 and RepEval 2017 workshops for their help and advice.

References

Jorge Balazs, Edison Marrese-Taylor, Pablo Loyola, and Yutaka Matsuo. 2017. Refining raw sentence representations for textual entailment recognition via attention. In *The Second Workshop on Evaluating Vector Space Representations for NLP (RepEval 2017)*.

Samuel R. Bowman, Gabor Angeli, Christopher Potts, and Christopher D. Manning. 2015. A large annotated corpus for learning natural language inference. In *Proc. EMNLP*.

Qian Chen, Xiaodan Zhu, Zhen-Hua Ling, Si Wei, Hui Jiang, and Diana Inkpen. 2017a. Enhanced LSTM for natural language inference. In *Proc. ACL*.

Qian Chen, Xiaodan Zhu, Zhen-Hua Ling, Si Wei, Hui Jiang, and Diana Inkpen. 2017b. Recurrent neural network-based sentence encoder with gated attention for natural language inference. In *Proceedings of The Second Workshop on Evaluating Vector Space Representations for NLP (RepEval 2017)*.

Gennaro Chierchia and Sally McConnell-Ginet. 1991. *Meaning and Grammar*. MIT Press, Cambridge, MA.

Alexis Conneau, Douwe Kiela, Holger Schwenk, Loïc Barrault, and Antoine Bordes. 2017. Supervised learning of universal sentence representations from natural language inference data. In *Proc. EMNLP*.

Ido Dagan, Oren Glickman, and Bernardo Magnini. 2006. The PASCAL recognising textual entailment challenge. In *Machine learning challenges. Evaluating predictive uncertainty, visual object classification, and recognising textual entailment*, Springer.

Sepp Hochreiter and Jürgen Schmidhuber. 1997. Long short-term memory. *Neural computation* 9(8).

Yoon Kim, Yacine Jernite, David Sontag, and Alexander M. Rush. 2016. Character-aware neural language models. In *Proc. AAAI*.

Bill MacCartney. 2009. *Natural Language Inference*. Ph.D. thesis, Stanford University.

Yixin Nie and Mohit Bansal. 2017. Shortcut-stacked sentence encoders for multi-domain inference. In *Proceedings of The Second Workshop on Evaluating Vector Space Representations for NLP (RepEval 2017)*.

Jeffrey Pennington, Richard Socher, and Christopher D. Manning. 2014. GloVe: Global vectors for word representation. In *Proc. EMNLP*.

Tim Rocktäschel, Edward Grefenstette, Karl Moritz Hermann, Tomáš Kočiský, and Phil Blunsom. 2016. Reasoning about entailment with neural attention. In *Proc. ICLR*.

Hoa Trong Vu, Thuong-Hai Pham, Xiaoyu Bai Marc Tanti, Lonneke van der Plas, and Albert Gatt. 2017. LCT-MALTA's submission to RepEval 2017 shared task. In *Proceedings of The Second Workshop on Evaluating Vector Space Representations for NLP (RepEval 2017)*.

Shuohang Wang and Jing Jiang. 2016. Learning natural language inference with LSTM. In *Proc. NAACL*.

Adina Williams, Nikita Nangia, and Samuel R. Bowman. 2017. A broad-coverage challenge corpus for sentence understanding through inference. *CoRR* abs/1704.05426.

Han Yang, Marta R. Costa-jussà, and José A. R. Fonollosa. 2017. Character-level intra attention network for natural language inference. In *Proceedings of The Second Workshop on Evaluating Vector Space Representations for NLP (RepEval 2017)*.

Traversal-Free Word Vector Evaluation in Analogy Space

Xiaoyin Che, Nico Ring, Willi Raschkowski, Haojin Yang, Christoph Meinel
Hasso Plattner Institute, University of Potsdam
Campus Griebnitzsee, D-14440 Potsdam, Germany
{xiaoyin.che, haojin.yang, christoph.meinel}@hpi.de
{nico.ring, willi.raschkowskil}@student.hpi.uni-potsdam.de

Abstract

In this paper, we propose an alternative evaluating metric for word analogy questions (*A to B is as C to D*) in word vector evaluation. Different from the traditional method which predicts the fourth word by the given three, we measure the similarity directly on the "relations" of two pairs of given words, just as shifting the relation vectors into a new analogy space. Cosine and Euclidean distances are then calculated as measurements. Observation and experiments shows the proposed analogy space evaluation could offer a more comprehensive evaluating result on word vectors with word analogy questions. Meanwhile, computational complexity are remarkably reduced by avoiding traversing the vocabulary.

1 Introduction

In recent years, word vector, or addressed as word embedding or distributed vector representation of word, achieves high popularity in NLP (***N**atural **L**anguage **P**rocessing*) applications. A word vector is a real-valued vector, which is quite low-dimensional when comparing with traditional one-hot representation of words. The theory behind is believed to be the early concept of distributional representation (Hinton, 1986), and modern word vector derives from the training process of neural language models (Bengio et al., 2003).

The usage of word vectors has been proven highly efficient and successful by various NLP tasks (Collobert et al., 2011), which further spurs the technical developments to achieve word vectors with better quality, such as Word2Vec (Mikolov et al., 2013a), GloVe (Pennington et al., 2014), Word2Vecf (Levy and Goldberg, 2014), LexVec (Salle et al., 2016), FastText (Bojanowski et al., 2016), *etc*.

However, discussion about how to evaluate the quality of word vectors remains open. Except for actual applications, most frequently used evaluation tasks are word similarity and word analogy. A word similarity task is to find the nearest word in the vector space of the given word, based on the theory that words with similar meanings should gather together. Although it is widely used, arguments are made to question its capability (Batchkarov et al., 2016; Faruqui et al., 2016).

While in a word analogy test, three words A, B and C are given and the goal is to find a fourth word D, which logically conforms "A to B is as C to D". Word analogy test has a long history of being used in examinations or IQ tests for human (McClelland, 1973; Sternberg, 1985) and is introduced into word vector evaluation by Mikolov *et al.* (2013b). After that, it has been widely applied.

Efforts are made to improve the original analogy metric, such as using PAIRDIRECTION to replace 3COSADD in calculation (Levy et al., 2014) or taking multiple word pairs into consideration (Drozd et al., 2016), but the goal is still to find word D from the vocabulary. Besides, Linzen (2016) made a thorough assessment of word analogy test, and the most prominent finding is that if not exclude three given words, the prediction of D would almost always be C (91%) or B (5%), especially when the lineal offset between words is small. This phenomenon would arouse the doubt, that whether we are searching for a word D which holds the same logic to C just as B to A, or actually searching for the nearest word of C? Furthermore, the general accuracy decline in reversed analogy also suggests the incertainty of current analogy evaluation metric.

In this paper, we would dig deeper into the limitations of current analogy evaluation metric in

Proceedings of the 2nd Workshop on Evaluating Vector-Space Representations for NLP, pages 11–15,
Copenhagen, Denmark, September 7–11, 2017. ©2017 Association for Computational Linguistics

Table 1: Examples of Traditional Word Analogy Evaluation Result (Words in order of A, B, C & D)

Grammar-1	knowing		knew		selling		sold	
Predictions	thought	0.573	know	0.481	purchased	0.520	**sold**	**0.568**
	know	0.504	**knew**	**0.449**	resold	0.506	sell	0.535
	wanted	0.494	Knowing	0.441	**selling**	**0.486**	bought	0.528
	knowing	0.489	figured	0.404	sale	0.484	buying	0.486
Grammar-2	looking		looked		shrinking		shrank	
Predictions	look	0.540	**looked**	**0.536**	**shrinking**	**0.560**	shrunk	0.618
	looking	**0.526**	look	0.493	unexpectedly_shrank	0.478	**shrank**	**0.589**
	looks	0.521	looks	0.415	downwardly_revised	0.468	dwindled	0.498
	seemed	0.439	expecting	0.410	contraction	0.454	shrink	0.498

Section 2 and propose our simple alternative plan in Section 3, which is called "Analogy Space Evaluation". A significant difference of our approach is that we avoid traversing vocabulary from time to time. Experiments are presented in Section 4 and finally come the conclusion and discussion.

2 Limitations of Traditional Metric

In traditional word analogy evaluation, by given word pairs (A, B) and (C, D) with same syntactic or semantic relation, the goal is to find the nearest word to "$C+B-A$" in the vector space by Cosine similarity and check whether the word obtained is D. Practically some approaches use unit vector of A, B and C in "$C+B-A$", such as widely used Word2Vec. Anyway, the return value of such a word analogy question is in Boolean type.

Generally, evaluating word vectors requires thousands of word analogy questions, which return thousands of Boolean values to calculate the accuracy from a macro perspective: how many supposed D have been successfully predicted. However, if we treat each question as an independent target in a micro aspect, result in Boolean type suffers an unneglectable information loss: true or false cannot quantitatively manifest the extent of how true or how false. For instance, it does not matter whether D is the 2nd nearest word to "$C+B-A$" or the 100th.

Another limitation of traditional metric is the deficiency in comprehensiveness. In a typical "A to B is as C to D" analogy, there are in fact 4 prediction choices, although in some analogies like "Nation-Currency" or "Nation-Language", available choices could drop to 2, since in reverse logic the answer is not unique. A single prediction on D is not enough to represent the quality of all 4 word vectors trained.

For better illustration, we run widely used "GoogleNews-vectors-negative300.bin" on default Word2Vec English analogy test and extract two examples to Table 1. All 4 words in example analogy questions are predicted and top 4 results are presented accordingly. From Table 1, it is clear that no matter with absolute value or average ranking of desired word in predictions, situation in Grammar-2 is apparently better than Grammar-1. However, because only word D is predicted by traditional metric, Grammar-1 would return a positive result while Grammar-2 is negative, which obviously fails to correctly represent the quality of corresponding word vectors trained.

In default Word2Vec analogy test, there is always another analogy question, which in fact predict word B of the original question. But there is no reverse logic prediction for A and C. So in final accuracy calculation, these two sets of words in Table 1 contribute the same precision of 0.5, which still cannot reflect the quality difference between these two sets of word vectors trained. Perhaps, 4 analogy questions are needed, but that would lead to another issue: higher complexity. Every time when searching for a nearest word, cosine similarity must be calculated with each word in the vocabulary. When the testing set is large, it may take quite a long time, and the time would be doubled if all 4 possible questions are included. Moreover, the majority of words in the vocabulary are actually unrelated with the prediction target. Calculating these words is simply wasting time.

Based on all above reasons, we aim to offer an alternative metric for word analogy evaluation, by constructing a new analogy space based on the relation vectors achieved from analogy questions, in order to solve existing limitations in quantification, comprehensiveness and complexity.

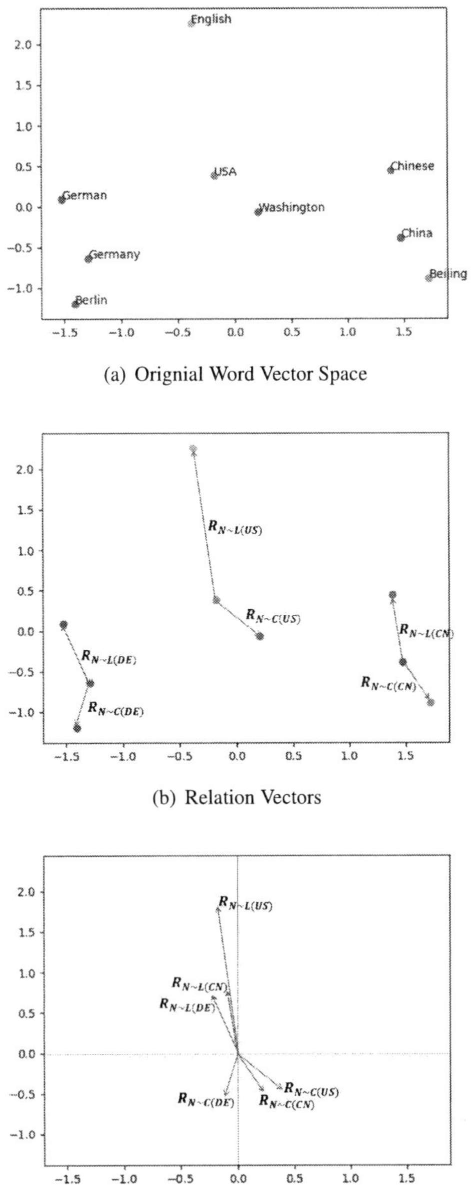

(a) Orignial Word Vector Space

(b) Relation Vectors

(c) Final Analogy Space

Figure 1: Analogy Space Illustration

Table 2: Analogy Space Evaluation (Micro)

Analogy	Cos.	Euc.	N-Cos.	N-Euc.
Grammar-1	0.114	0.334	0.115	0.332
Grammar-2	0.324	0.410	0.320	0.415
NC: US-CN	0.310	0.380	0.314	0.356
NC: US-DE	0.367	0.423	0.376	0.411
NC: DE-CN	0.496	0.492	0.508	0.495
NL: US-CN	0.452	0.420	0.451	0.405
NL: US-DE	0.438	0.430	0.441	0.418
NL: DE-CN	0.712	0.617	0.714	0.619

3 Analogy Space Evaluation

Proposed analogy space shares same dimensionality of original word vector space. For each analogy question, two relation vectors can be found in original word vector space, just as the definition of PAIRDIRECTION by Levy *et al.* (2014). Mathematically, the value of such a relation vector is the same as the position of the ending point if we take the starting point as the space origin. This is simply the new analogy space: shifting all relation vectors to the space origin, so each point in this new space represents a relation between a pair of words given in the analogy question. Figure 1 illustrates this process by several example words of "Nation-Capital" and "Nation-Language" analogies (*extracted from same test of Table 1, visualized by PCA*).

Naturally, we expect relations with same or similar logic gather together in the analogy space. In order to quantitatively evaluate the similarity, we prepare four different measurements, based on Cosine similarity or Euclidean distance respectively. If we denote the vectors of word A, B, C and D as $\mathbf{a}$, $\mathbf{b}$, $\mathbf{c}$ and $\mathbf{d}$, then

$$Cos. = \frac{(\mathbf{b}-\mathbf{a})\cdot(\mathbf{d}-\mathbf{c})}{\|\mathbf{b}-\mathbf{a}\|\|\mathbf{d}-\mathbf{c}\|} \tag{1}$$

$$Euc. = 1 - \frac{\|(\mathbf{b}-\mathbf{a})-(\mathbf{d}-\mathbf{c})\|}{\|\mathbf{b}-\mathbf{a}\|+\|\mathbf{d}-\mathbf{c}\|} \tag{2}$$

while $Cos. \in [-1,1]$ and $Euc. \in [0,1]$. *N-Cos.* and *N-Euc.* have similar definitions, but using unit word vectors in calculation. Table 2 shows the result of examples mentioned in Table 1 and Figure 1. Among them, "NC:DE-CN" and "NL:DE-CN" succeed 2/2 in traditional nearest word evaluation, while all others achieve 1/2.

It's clear that proposed measurements could better represent the quality of these involved words or relations in a quantitative way. As already mentioned, words in Grammar-2 are considered better trained than Grammar-1, and this difference can be captured by proposed measurements only. And for NCs and NLs, traditional metric reports exactly the same accuracy, but as we can see, detailed similarities differ a lot. We believe these phenomena could help word analogy evaluation in the micro aspect.

Table 3: Analogy Space Evaluation (Macro)

WV Set	Voc.	Traditional		Proposed					SBD	
		Accu.	Time	Cos.	Euc.	N-Cos.	N-Euc.	Time	4C	2C
EN-w5-i5	1.8M	0.697	24'56"	0.325	0.419	0.325	0.420	0'38"	0.575	0.820
EN-w10-i10	1.8M	0.692	24'41"	0.314	0.414	0.315	0.415	0'37"	0.573	0.822
GoogleNews	3M	0.737	30'48"	0.352	0.431	0.352	0.431	1'09"	0.580	0.824
DE-w5-cbow	1.8M	0.465	92'39"	0.324	0.418	0.335	0.423	1'33"	–	–
DE-w5-sg	1.8M	0.434	92'09"	0.259	0.389	0.260	0.392	1'35"	–	–
DE-w10-cbow	1.8M	0.463	89'22"	0.318	0.416	0.331	0.422	1'37"	0.640	0.779
DE-w10-sg	1.8M	0.412	94'13"	0.251	0.385	0.254	0.389	1'34"	0.619	0.767

4 Macro Experiments

In this section, we would do some experiments on complete analogy question sets and discuss complexity. For English word vectors, we trained two sets on Wikipedia dump with different window size (*w*) and iteration (*i*) by Skip-Gram model, with same dimensionality of 300. They would further be compared with GoogleNews public set. We will evaluate these sets with proposed measurements, along with traditional analogy evaluation result and the performances of a downstream application: *Sentence **Boundary** **Detection** (SBD)*. Details of SBD implementation can be found in references (Che et al., 2016a,b).

Beside of English test, we also conducted several tests in German. Leipzig dataset (Goldhahn et al., 2012) are used to training German word vectors with Word2Vec toolkit. Then the vectors with different training configurations are evaluated by a set of analogy questions, which contains 2834 semantic questions in 18 categories (*including some reverse logics*) and 77886 syntactic questions in 9 categories. We have uploaded these analogy questions in German for public access[1].

Table 3 shows the results and time expenditures of these experiments. It is clear that proposed measurements have same trend with traditional metric, which means once set X achieves better result than set Y in traditional test, it would also do better in proposed alternatives. Performances in downstream application SBD are also fit this trend in general. Meanwhile, proposed evaluation could significantly save time, approximately 95%. These facts prove that we can achieve same performance within way less time.

However, we also found some limitations. The absolute difference between different vector sets in proposed measurements is smaller, which make it difficult to distinguish, especially with *Euc.* and *N-Euc.* It is also unclear that which measurement from the four proposed could be the optimized option.

[1]https://drive.google.com/open?id=0B13Cc1a7ebTuaE83NEtyemM4aGM

5 Conclusion & Discussion

In this paper, we discuss some limitations of traditional word analogy evaluation metric in word vector evaluation, and then propose a simple alternative plan called "Analogy Space Evaluation", which directly measures the relation vectors between given pairs of words, instead of traversing the vocabulary to seek the nearest word of the target. Experiments shows that proposed approach serves as good as traditional metric in performance, but reduces the computational complexity significantly.

This effort can be simply applied on any existing word analogy tasks. Frankly speaking, we cannot claim that our method outperforms the original, except for the complexity part. But complexity does matter. Currently analogy tasks generally contain tens of thousands questions, so traditional traversal-based evaluation can still manage. However, we would definitely want to test higher portion of words in the vocabulary, and with the efforts from the whole community, we may have a "nearly optimized" test set someday with up to million words involved. At that time, traversal-free could be a highly desirable quality.

As far as we know, there is no widely acknowledged benchmark which can be used to test new evaluation methods, so our effort remains estimation. In the future, we would attempt to implement more real applications, just as SBD mentioned in this paper, and take their performances as feedbacks, in order to contribute in this dilemma of "Evaluation of Evaluation".

References

Miroslav Batchkarov, Thomas Kober, Jeremy Reffin, Julie Weeds, and David Weir. 2016. A critique of word similarity as a method for evaluating distributional semantic models .

Yoshua Bengio, Réjean Ducharme, Pascal Vincent, and Christian Jauvin. 2003. A neural probabilistic language model. *Journal of machine learning research* 3(Feb):1137–1155.

Piotr Bojanowski, Edouard Grave, Armand Joulin, and Tomas Mikolov. 2016. Enriching word vectors with subword information. *arXiv preprint arXiv:1607.04606* .

Xiaoyin Che, Sheng Luo, Haojin Yang, and Christoph Meinel. 2016a. Sentence boundary detection based on parallel lexical and acoustic models. *Interspeech 2016* pages 2528–2532.

Xiaoyin Che, Cheng Wang, Haojin Yang, and Christoph Meinel. 2016b. Punctuation prediction for unsegmented transcript based on word vector. In *The 10th International Conference on Language Resources and Evaluation (LREC)*.

Ronan Collobert, Jason Weston, Léon Bottou, Michael Karlen, Koray Kavukcuoglu, and Pavel Kuksa. 2011. Natural language processing (almost) from scratch. *Journal of Machine Learning Research* 12(Aug):2493–2537.

Aleksandr Drozd, Anna Gladkova, and Satoshi Matsuoka. 2016. Word embeddings, analogies, and machine learning: Beyond king - man + woman = queen. *Proceedings of COLING 2016, the 26th International Conference on Computational Linguistics: Technical Papers,* pages 3519–3530.

Manaal Faruqui, Yulia Tsvetkov, Pushpendre Rastogi, and Chris Dyer. 2016. Problems with evaluation of word embeddings using word similarity tasks. *arXiv preprint arXiv:1605.02276* .

Dirk Goldhahn, Thomas Eckart, and Uwe Quasthoff. 2012. Building large monolingual dictionaries at the leipzig corpora collection: From 100 to 200 languages. In *LREC*. pages 759–765.

Geoffrey E Hinton. 1986. Learning distributed representations of concepts. In *Proceedings of the eighth annual conference of the cognitive science society*. Amherst, MA, volume 1, page 12.

Omer Levy and Yoav Goldberg. 2014. Dependency-based word embeddings. In *Proceedings of the 52nd Annual Meeting of the Association for Computational Linguistics, Volume 2.*. The Association for Computer Linguistics.

Omer Levy, Yoav Goldberg, and Israel Ramat-Gan. 2014. Linguistic regularities in sparse and explicit word representations. In *CoNLL*. pages 171–180.

Tal Linzen. 2016. Issues in evaluating semantic spaces using word analogies. *arXiv preprint arXiv:1606.07736* .

David C McClelland. 1973. Testing for competence rather than for" intelligence.". *American psychologist* 28(1):1.

Tomas Mikolov, Kai Chen, Greg Corrado, and Jeffrey Dean. 2013a. Efficient estimation of word representations in vector space. *arXiv preprint arXiv:1301.3781* .

Tomas Mikolov, Wen-tau Yih, and Geoffrey Zweig. 2013b. Linguistic regularities in continuous space word representations. In *HLT-NAACL*. pages 746–751.

Jeffrey Pennington, Richard Socher, and Christopher D Manning. 2014. Glove: Global vectors for word representation. *Proceedings of the Empiricial Methods in Natural Language Processing (EMNLP 2014)* 12:1532–1543.

Alexandre Salle, Marco Idiart, and Aline Villavicencio. 2016. Matrix factorization using window sampling and negative sampling for improved word representations. In *The 54th Annual Meeting of the Association for Computational Linguistics*. page 419.

Robert J Sternberg. 1985. *Beyond IQ: A triarchic theory of human intelligence*. CUP Archive.

Hypothesis Testing based Intrinsic Evaluation of Word Embeddings

Nishant Gurnani
Department of Mathematics
University of California San Diego
ndgurnan@ucsd.edu

Abstract

We introduce the cross-match test - an exact, distribution free, high-dimensional hypothesis test as an intrinsic evaluation metric for word embeddings. We show that cross-match is an effective means of measuring distributional similarity between different vector representations and of evaluating the statistical significance of different vector embedding models. Additionally, we find that cross-match can be used to provide a quantitative measure of linguistic similarity for selecting bridge languages for machine translation. We demonstrate that the results of the hypothesis test align with our expectations and note that the framework of two sample hypothesis testing is not limited to word embeddings and can be extended to all vector representations.

1 Introduction

Word embeddings obtained via specialized models (Brown et al., 1992; Pennington et al., 2014; Mikolov et al., 2013a) or neural networks (Bengio et al., 2003) have been successfully used to address various natural language processing tasks (Vaswani et al., 2013; Soricut and Och, 2015). These embeddings provide a nuanced representation of words that can capture various syntactic and semantic properties of natural language (Mikolov et al., 2013b). Despite their effectiveness in downstream applications, embeddings have limited practical value as standalone items. Consequently, an intrinsic evaluation metric must provide insight on the downstream task the embeddings are designed for. In this work, we use Cross-match (Rosenbaum, 2005) - an exact, distribution free, high-dimensional hypothesis test to propose a novel approach for intrinsic evaluation of word embeddings, one that provides insight on tasks that depend on linguistic similarity.

Evaluating general purpose vector representations is difficult. They are trained using simple objectives and applied to a variety of downstream tasks, thus making no single extrinsic evaluation definitive. Often, due to computational constraints, direct downstream evaluations are also impractical. In the case of word embeddings, these constraints have led to the development of dedicated evaluation tasks like similarity and analogy (Rohde et al., 2006; Levy et al., 2015) which are not directly related to training objectives or to downstream tasks. Despite their ease of interpretability, Faruqui et al. (2016) have shown that these tasks do not correlate well with downstream performance. In related work, Tsvetkov et al. (2016) propose an evaluation measure QVEC-CCA that is shown to correlate well with downstream semantic tasks where the objective is to quantify the linguistic content of word embeddings by maximizing the correlation with a manually annotated linguistic resource.

In this work, we use the Cross-match hypothesis test (Rosenbaum, 2005) to measure distributional similarity between different word vector representations. Cross-match is an adjacency based test traditionally used in clinical settings where the goal is to assess no treatment effect on a high-dimensional outcome in a randomized experiment. In our setting, we assume there exists some unknown distribution W from which our constructed word embeddings $\{\mathbf{w_1}, \ldots, \mathbf{w_n}\}$ are "sampled" from. Given two sets of word embeddings, cross-match tests whether the underlying distribution from which the embeddings were "sampled" are identical or not. The test uses optimal non-bipartite matching to pair vectors from both sets of embeddings based on distance (e.g.

Proceedings of the 2nd Workshop on Evaluating Vector-Space Representations for NLP, pages 16–20,
Copenhagen, Denmark, September 7–11, 2017. ©2017 Association for Computational Linguistics

a vector will be paired with it's nearest neighbor based on some distance metric). The cross-match test statistic C is the number of times that a vector from one set is paired with a vector from another. The null hypothesis assumes that the vectors were sampled from the same distribution and rejects for small values of C. Thus, a large number of cross-matches between two sets of word embeddings suggests that they are from the same embedding distribution.

Using cross-match, we propose two illustrative examples of intrinsic evaluation. First, we use pretrained word vectors (trained on Wikipedia using the skip-gram model in Bojanowski et al. (2016)) from Facebook's fastText library for several languages to calculate the cross-match statistic for several language pairs. We hypothesize that for linguistically similar languages, a larger statistic will be observed. Secondly, we use cross-match to assess the statistical significant of word embedding models. We consider several well known models trained on the same corpus and use cross-match to assess whether the respective word vector representations are statistically significantly different. We hypothesize that the number of cross-matches between two different embedding models is small, thus suggesting that they capture fundamentally different linguistic aspects of the corpus.

This paper is organized as follows: Section 2 introduces the cross-match test in detail. Experiments on embedding similarity and evaluation are described in Section 3. We discuss extensions and conclude in Section 4.

2 Cross-Match Test

The cross-match test (Rosenbaum, 2005) is a nonparametric goodness-of-fit test in arbitrary dimensions. It is an exact, distribution-free, two-sample hypothesis test that measures whether two distributions are equal or not. Formally, given two independent samples $w_1, \ldots, w_n \sim W$ and $v_1, \ldots, v_m \sim V$, cross-match tests the null hypothesis $H_0 : W = V$ versus the alternative hypothesis $H_1 : W \neq V$. The test has been traditionally used in clinical settings, where the goal is to assess no treatment effect on a high-dimensional outcome between control and treated subjects in a randomized experiment (Heller et al., 2010). In the case of word embeddings, the goal is to test whether two sets of word embedding vectors have been "sampled" from the same distribution.

2.1 Definition of the Cross-Match Statistic

Let W, V denote two word embedding distributions (distributions of word embedding vectors over a corpus), suppose we obtain two sets of word vectors $\{\mathbf{w_1}, \ldots, \mathbf{w_n}\} \sim W$ and $\{\mathbf{v_1}, \ldots, \mathbf{v_m}\} \sim V$. Assign the group labels 0 and 1 to indicate which sample the vectors are from such that the data are organized as follows: $\{(0, \mathbf{w_1}), \ldots, (0, \mathbf{w_n})\}$ and $\{(1, \mathbf{v_1}), \ldots (1, \mathbf{v_m})\}$.

The cross-match statistic C, is a function of the word vectors $D = \{\mathbf{w_1}, \ldots, \mathbf{w_n}, \mathbf{v_1}, \ldots, \mathbf{v_n}\}$ and the group labels $G = \{0, \ldots, 0, 1, \ldots, 1\}$. If $H_0 : W = V$ is true, then all the word vectors are i.i.d. "sampled" from W and the group labels are meaningless. It's as if the 0's and 1's were randomly assigned.

The cross-match test is performed as follows. For notational convenience ignore the group labels and treat the data as one sample $\{\mathbf{z_1}, \ldots, \mathbf{z_{n+m}}\}$ of size $n+m = N$ (assume for simplicity that N is even). We define a $N \times N$ symmetric distance matrix, with row k and column l giving the distance (any distance metric can be used) between $\mathbf{z_k}$ and $\mathbf{z_l}$. Compute the optimal non-bipartite matching of the $\mathbf{z}'\mathbf{s}$ (match the vectors into non-overlapping pairs) that minimizes the total distances between the points in each pair.

Formally, we find a permutation $\hat{\sigma}$ of $\{1, \ldots, N\}$ that minimizes

$$Match(\sigma) = \sum_{i=1}^{N} d(Z_i, Z_{\sigma(i)})$$

where $i \neq \sigma(i)$ and d is our chosen distance measure. The cross-match statistic C, is defined as the number of pairs that have group labels (0,1) or (1,0), the test rejects for small values of C.

If there is an odd number of word embedding vectors, then a psuedo-vector is added to the distance matrix at zero distance from everyone else. $\frac{N}{2}$ pairs are formed as before, and the pair containing the psuedo-vector is discarded (thus the least matchable word vector is discarded).

2.2 Null Distribution of the Cross-Match Statistic

One advantage of the cross-match test is that we can compute the exact distribution of the statistic C under the null hypothesis H_0. Given $\frac{N}{2}$ paired vectors, let c_0 denote the observed number of the pairs with group labels (0,0), let c_1 denote the observed number of pairs with group labels (0,1) or (1,0) (this is our observed cross-match statistic) and finally let c_2 denote the observed number of pairs with group labels (1,1). The null distribution of C in closed form is:

$$f(c_1) = P(C = c_1) = \frac{2^{c_1} n!}{\binom{N}{n} c_0! c_1! c_2!}$$

where $\frac{N}{2} = c_0 + c_1 + c_2$. Having the null distribution in closed form also allows us to compute the exact p-value for our observed cross-match statistic. The resulting p-value is equal to $F(c_1)$ where

$$F(c_1) = P(C \leq c_1) = \sum_{c_1'=0}^{c_1} f(c_1')$$

A low p-value would suggests that we have evidence to reject the null hypothesis (at a given level of significance) that the word embedding vectors were "sampled" from the same distribution.

3 Experiments

In the following experiments, we demonstrate two different illustrative examples of the cross-match test. Our objective is to show the effectiveness of cross-match as a general tool for intrinsic evaluation of word embedding vectors.

3.1 Embedding Similarity

A bridge language (also referred to as a pivot language), is an artificial or natural language used as an intermediary for translation between two different languages. In machine translation, a bridge language is useful in low-resource situations where a good parallel corpora is not available for the target language. In such cases, a resource rich, linguistically similar language is used as a proxy in order to perform the required NLP task. For example in Tsvetkov and Dyer (2015) the authors use Arabic, Italian and French as bridge languages to perform Swahili-English, Maltese-English and Romanian-English translations respectively.

Assessing whether languages are linguistically similar is a reasonably difficult task and depends on the notion of similarity one uses (lexical, morphological etc.) In this experiment, we use cross-match to provide a quantitative measure to assess linguistic similarity between languages.

We use pre-trained word vectors (trained on Wikipedia using the skip-gram model in Bojanowski et al. (2016)) from Facebook's fastText library for several languages and calculate the cross-match statistic for several language pairs. Specifically, we randomly select 100,000 word vectors for each language (with the exception of Maltese and Swahili which have only 26,000 and 52,000 vectors respectively). Then for each language pair, we randomly sample 200 vectors and calculate the number of cross-matches between them using R's crossmatch package (`https://github.com/cran/crossmatch`). We repeat this 500 times for each language pair and report the average cross-match statistic.

Language Pair	Cross-Match
English-French	23.76
English-Italian	25.04
English-Spanish	23.36
English-Portuguese	18.44
English-Arabic	19.34
English-Maltese	7.84
English-Romanian	16.56
English-Swahili	17

Table 1: fastText vectors cross-match statistics for English-pair languages

Language Pair	Cross-Match
Maltese-English	7.84
Maltese-French	7.28
Maltese-Italian	9.20
Maltese-Spanish	6.76
Maltese-Portuguese	4.84
Maltese-Arabic	6.68
Maltese-Romanian	6.96
Maltese-Swahili	4.44

Table 2: fastText vectors cross-match statistics for Maltese-pair languages

Tables 1 and 2 present the results of calculating the average number of cross-matches between several English-pair and Maltese-pair languages. We note that with a sample of 400 vectors (200 from each language) the maximum possible number of cross-matches is 200. Given that are our reported statistics are considerably lower than 200 we can safely conclude that the distributions from which the word embedding vectors were generated are different for different languages. In table 1 we note that the number of cross-matches between English and other romance languages (French, Italian, Spanish, Portuguese, Romanian) is noticeably higher than that between English and non-romance languages (Arabic, Maltese, Swahili). This corresponds with our notions of linguistic similarity between the languages, we certainly expect English to be more "similar" to French than to Maltese. We also note that in table 2, the Maltese-Italian pair has the highest cross-match statistic, thus supporting the choice of Italian as a bridge language for Maltese.

3.2 Embedding Evaluation

In this experiment, we use cross-match to assess the statistical significance of word embedding models. Despite the popularity of various different embedding models (Mikolov et al., 2013a,b; Pennington et al., 2014) it is not always clear whether one model represents a statistically significant improvement to other existing models (it maybe that all of them capture largely similar features of the text).

We consider four popular word embedding models: word2vec Skip-gram, word2vec CBOW, Glove and fastText all trained on the same English wikipedia corpus. Once again we take samples of size 200 from each method, caluclate the p-value between two pairs of methods using cross-match and then report the average p-value across 500 repeated iterations.

	Skip	CBOW	Glove	FastText
Skip	-	4.93e-26	2.39e-27	1.66e-23
CBOW	4.93e-26	-	9.42e-25	2.71e-22
Glove	2.39e-27	9.42e-25	-	1.13e-23
fastText	1.66e-23	2.71e-22	1.13e-23	-

Table 3: p-values calculated using Cross-match

The results in 3 show low p-values across all pairs of word embedding methods thus suggesting that they all seem to capture different aspects of the corpus they are modeling. In other words, using cross-match we have evidence to reject the null hypothesis that the vectors derived from any pair of models come from the same word embedding distribution.

Lastly, we note that there are at present some computational constraints in performing the cross-match test. There exists a bottleneck in the calculation of the optimal non-bipartite matching and this makes performing the test for larger sample sizes currently intractable. However, we feel confident that this software issue can be easily overcome by writing custom routines (as opposed to using existing open-source code) and parallelizing the problem. As a result of our limited sample size, we not that it is possible that the power of our hypothesis test is low and thus we may be making type I errors (falsely rejecting the null). Nonetheless our initial results seem promising and are in line with our expectations.

4 Conclusion

In this work we introduced the cross-match test, an exact, distribution free, high-dimensional hypothesis test as an intrinsic evaluation metric for word embeddings. We were able to demonstrate on two illustrative examples that the test performs reasonably in line with our expectations and can potentially be a useful tool in assessing bridge languages for machine translation. Despite the initially promising results, much further work remains to be done in order to confirm the efficacy of cross-match in the context of word embeddings.

We posit that our main contribution is the introduction of the hypothesis testing framework as a method for intrinsic evaluation of vector representations. We observe that there is nothing notable about word embeddings or the cross-match test and our experiments could be extended for other vector representations (sentence, phrase etc.) using other modern two-sample hypothesis tests such as the popular maximum mean discrepancy (Gretton et al., 2012). Given the rich literature on hypothesis testing in statistics, there is certainly much to be explored here.

For future work we aim to focus solely on the problem of bridge languages in machine translation. Our objective is to conduct a larger scale study that is able to definitively show a strong correlation between the results of a hypothesis test on word embedding vectors, and their subsequent performance on the downstream machine translation task.

Acknowledgments

We thank Ndapa Nakashole for several useful discussions helping formulate the problem and the anonymous reviewers for their feedback.

References

Yoshua Bengio, Réjean Ducharme, Pascal Vincent, and Christian Janvin. 2003. A neural probabilistic language model. *J. Mach. Learn. Res.* 3:1137–1155.

Piotr Bojanowski, Edouard Grave, Armand Joulin, and Tomas Mikolov. 2016. Enriching word vectors with subword information. *arXiv preprint arXiv:1607.04606* .

Peter F. Brown, Peter V. deSouza, Robert L. Mercer, Vincent J. Della Pietra, and Jenifer C. Lai. 1992. Class-based n-gram models of natural language. *Comput. Linguist.* 18(4):467–479.

Manaal Faruqui, Yulia Tsvetkov, Pushpendre Rastogi, and Chris Dyer. 2016. Problems with evaluation of word embeddings using word similarity tasks. *CoRR* abs/1605.02276.

Arthur Gretton, Karsten M. Borgwardt, Malte J. Rasch, Bernhard Schölkopf, and Alexander Smola. 2012. A kernel two-sample test. *J. Mach. Learn. Res.* 13:723–773.

Ruth Heller, Shane T. Jensen, Paul R. Rosenbaum, and Dylan S. Small. 2010. Sensitivity analysis for the cross-match test, with applications in genomics. *Journal of the American Statistical Association* 105(491):1005–1013.

Omer Levy, Yoav Goldberg, and Ido Dagan. 2015. Improving distributional similarity with lessons learned from word embeddings. *Transactions of the Association for Computational Linguistics* 3:211–225.

Tomas Mikolov, Kai Chen, Greg Corrado, and Jeffrey Dean. 2013a. Efficient estimation of word representations in vector space. *CoRR* abs/1301.3781.

Tomas Mikolov, Ilya Sutskever, Kai Chen, Greg S Corrado, and Jeff Dean. 2013b. Distributed representations of words and phrases and their compositionality. In C. J. C. Burges, L. Bottou, M. Welling, Z. Ghahramani, and K. Q. Weinberger, editors, *Advances in Neural Information Processing Systems 26*, pages 3111–3119.

Jeffrey Pennington, Richard Socher, and Christopher D Manning. 2014. Glove: Global vectors for word representation. In *EMNLP*. volume 14, pages 1532–1543.

Douglas L. T. Rohde, Laura M. Gonnerman, and David C. Plaut. 2006. An improved model of semantic similarity based on lexical co-occurence. *COMMUNICATIONS OF THE ACM* 8:627–633.

Paul R. Rosenbaum. 2005. An exact distribution-free test comparing two multivariate distributions based on adjacency. *Journal of the Royal Statistical Society: Series B (Statistical Methodology)* 67(4):515–530.

Radu Soricut and Franz Och. 2015. Unsupervised morphology induction using word embeddings. In *Proceedings of the 2015 Conference of the North American Chapter of the Association for Computational Linguistics: Human Language Technologies*. Association for Computational Linguistics, Denver, Colorado, pages 1627–1637.

Yulia Tsvetkov and Chris Dyer. 2015. Cross-lingual bridges with models of lexical borrowing. *J. Artif. Intell. Res. (JAIR)* 55:63–93.

Yulia Tsvetkov, Manaal Faruqui, and Chris Dyer. 2016. Correlation-based intrinsic evaluation of word vector representations. *CoRR* abs/1606.06710.

Ashish Vaswani, Yinggong Zhao, Victoria Fossum, and David Chiang. 2013. Decoding with large-scale neural language models improves translation. In *EMNLP*. ACL, pages 1387–1392.

Evaluation of word embeddings against cognitive processes: primed reaction times in lexical decision and naming tasks

Jeremy Auguste[1], **Arnaud Rey**[2], **Benoit Favre**[1]
Aix-Marseille Université, CNRS
[1]LIF UMR 7279, [2]LPC UMR 7290
13000 Marseille, France
{firstname.lastname}@univ-amu.fr

Abstract

This work presents a framework for word similarity evaluation grounded on cognitive sciences experimental data. Word pair similarities are compared to reaction times of subjects in large scale lexical decision and naming tasks under semantic priming. Results show that GloVe embeddings lead to significantly higher correlation with experimental measurements than other controlled and off-the-shelf embeddings, and that the choice of a training corpus is less important than that of the algorithm. Comparison of rankings with other datasets shows that the cognitive phenomenon covers more aspects than simply word relatedness or similarity.

1 Introduction

Word representations have attracted a lot of interest in the community and led to very useful applications in a range of domains of natural language processing. Such representations are typically evaluated intrinsically on word similarity tasks and extrinsically on their impact on NLP systems performance (Schnabel et al., 2015; Lai et al., 2016; Ghannay et al., 2016).

A recent trend towards building more general representations has looked at how similarities in the representation space can predict the outcome of cognitive experiments, such as human reaction time in semantic priming experiments (Ettinger and Linzen, 2016) or relying on eye tracking and brain imaging data (Søgaard, 2016; Ruan et al., 2016). The idea is that ground truth from unconscious phenomena might be less prone to subjective factors of more traditional word similarity and relatedness datasets.

In this paper, we describe an evaluation framework based on comparing word embedding similarity against reaction times from the Semantic Priming Project (Hutchison et al., 2013). A set of word embeddings is evaluated by computing its Spearman rank correlation with average reaction times obtained by submitting a set of subjects to a prime (one word from the pair) and then perform one of two tasks: lexical decision (decide whether the second word is an existing word or not), and naming (read aloud the second word).

Extending the ideas developed in (Ettinger and Linzen, 2016), this paper describes the following contributions:

- we create and distribute a package[1] for word embedding evaluation based on the SPP primed reaction time data;
- in order to calibrate results from that evaluation framework, we look at the effect of training corpus on a set of word embeddings;
- we also look at the correlation between SPP reaction times and subjective similarity and relatedness ratings from existing datasets.

2 Related Work

Intrinsic and extrinsic approaches have been proposed for word embedding evaluation. The former typically consist in collecting human judgment of word similarity on a range of word pairs, and computing the rank correlation of their averaged value with the cosine similarity between the embeddings of the words in the pair. Word analogy is also evaluated but it has been proven to be equivalent to a linear combination between cosine similarities (Levy et al., 2014). In this work, we focus on

[1]Available at https://github.com/JomnTAL/spp-wordsim

Proceedings of the 2nd Workshop on Evaluating Vector-Space Representations for NLP, pages 21–26,
Copenhagen, Denmark, September 7–11, 2017. ©2017 Association for Computational Linguistics

intrinsic evaluation, and therefore do not detail efforts for extrinsic evaluation of word embeddings. More pointers can be found in (Schnabel et al., 2015; Lai et al., 2016; Ghannay et al., 2016).

A number of datasets can be used to evaluate word similarity based on human judgment. Older datasets, such as RG (Rubenstein and Goodenough, 1965) and MC (Miller and Charles, 1991) shall not be used because differences between correlations are not significant due to their small size (Faruqui et al., 2016). While early datasets contained judgments collected in-house, such as WS-353 (Finkelstein et al., 2001; Agirre et al., 2009), most recent ones are created through crowd sourcing, with 10 to 20 annotations per word-pair, filtered for outliers: MTurk-287 (Radinsky et al., 2011), MTurk-771 (Halawi et al., 2012), MEN (Bruni et al., 2012), RW (Luong et al., 2013). Another trend is to address different syntactic categories than noun, such as YP-130 (Yang and Powers, 2006) and Verb (Baker et al., 2014) which focus on verbs. While past studies did not differentiate relatedness from semantic similarity, SimLex (Hill et al., 2016) and SimVerb (Gerz et al., 2016) explicitly promote the later. Embeddings can also be compared to lexical resources (Tsvetkov et al., 2015), but it is hard to balance the contribution of each linguistic phenomenon. Existing similarity ratings are subjective because they are the result of a conscious process while it seems desirable to directly evaluate embeddings against basic processes that support language in the brain.

In the cognitive sciences community, there has been efforts to explain how word associations are formed by introducing word embeddings in models. Pereira et al. (2016) look at how off-the-shelf word embeddings predict free associations (given a prime, say the first word that comes to your mind), a conscious process while we are interested in an unconscious process. The work by Hollis and Westbury (2016), among other experiments, compares word embedding principal components to unprimed reaction times from the English Lexicon Project (ELP) and British Lexicon Project (BLP). Both papers are interested in explaining cognitive behavior. There have also been efforts to evaluate word embeddings against fMRI recordings with the idea that embeddings can explain part of the neural activity (Søgaard, 2016).

The work by Ettinger and Linzen (2016) is particularly relevant to our study in that the authors also propose to evaluate embeddings against reaction time data from the SPP dataset. Our work differs in that we provide an evaluation setup which can be reused by other researchers, we propose a different evaluation metric based on rank correlation, and we perform an analysis in regard to different parameters, in particular the corpus used to train embeddings.

3 Semantic priming

There is an extensive psychological literature concerning the nature of semantic representations and the influence of semantic or associative context on word processing (McNamara, 2005). In this domain, the semantic priming paradigm is one of the most popular experimental tool to study these cognitive processes. In this task, participants are presented with a prime (stimulus) word (e.g., cat) immediately followed by either a related (e.g., dog) or an unrelated (e.g., truck) target word. A speeded response is expected on the target word (e.g., a lexical-decision, i.e., is it a word or not?) and a response time is recorded. Semantic priming refers to the finding that people respond faster to target words preceded by related, relative to unrelated, primes. This behavioral index therefore provides information about the influence of a semantic context (i.e., the prime word) on the processing of the target word and is suitable for the development of theories of semantic memory.

Due to the increasing precision of computational models of word processing, researchers are now testing models by using large-scale databases providing experimental data at the item level. The Semantic Priming Project (SPP) (Hutchison et al., 2013) is one of these recently collected databases. It provides response times from 768 participants in speeded naming (NT) and lexical decision (LDT) tasks for 1,661 target words following related and unrelated primes. The naming task consists in reading aloud the target, while the lexical decision task consists in pressing one of two buttons to specify if the target is a valid word or not. Aside from the relatedness between the prime and the target, the item data is also available for stimulus onset asynchronies (SOA) between the prime and target items of 200 and 1,200 ms. Stimulus onset asynchrony is the time between the end of showing the first (stimulus) word, and the target word in the reaction time experiments. Semantic priming at shorter SOAs (e.g., under 300 ms) is thought to reflect automatic priming mechanisms, whereas priming at longer SOAs (e.g., over 300 ms) presumably reflects additional intentional strategies (Hutchison et al., 2001).

Reaction times observed in semantic priming experiments can be explained by a range of linguistic phenomena, such as relatedness, semantic similarity, syntactic traits, or morphology. Unlike Hill et al. (2016) who focus on one phenomenon, we assume that word representations should convey the full mixture of explaining factors observed in unplanned human behavior. Therefore we evaluate embeddings by computing the correlation between the cosine similarity of pairs of words and reaction times (RT). Shorter RT indicate more priming effect, leading to negative correlations. In addition, non linguistic factors such as frequency are known to influence RT measurements, so it is not expected that word embeddings explain the whole variance of the experiment.

The SPP data is significantly larger than word similarity datasets and consists of 6,637 word pairs. The RT for each pair is an average over the performance of 30 subjects. In addition to reaction times, the dataset contains demographics, proficiency and attention tests results.

4 Evaluation framework

Embeddings are evaluated by computing the cosine similarity between word pairs from the SPP project, and look at their Spearman rank correlation with the RT data. The results are given in term of negative correlation. Significance of the difference between correlations is calculated with the Steiger test (Steiger, 1980).

In this evaluation framework, the word pairs for the Lexical Decision Task (LDT) and Naming Task (NT) are split according to two partitions. The first one (P1), used here, consists of a development set of 1,328 pairs and a test set of 5,309 pairs. Parameters of the proposed approaches can be tuned on the development set and performance must be reported on the test set. Another partition (P2) is made available to also include data for training algorithms. The Train set consists of 3,981 pairs, the Dev has 1,328 pairs and the Test has 1,328 pairs. These partitions were obtained by using 10 folds which are also available. We didn't create them with a particular goal in mind but we made sure that the mean word frequency and the standard deviation (SD) of each fold was close to the mean word frequency and SD of the full dataset. By standardizing the data splits, we ensure that results presented in future work will be comparable.

Experiments In a first set of experiments, we benchmark a range of embeddings on the SPP data. Four conditions are considered: LDT-200, LDT-1200, NT-200, NT-1200 (for lexical decision task, and naming task, both with an onset of 200 ms and 1,200 ms). We compare two categories of embeddings: a controlled setting for which algorithms are trained on the same dataset, and a selection of pretrained embeddings available to the community. Due to space constraints, the pretrained embeddings considered[2] are limited to: W2V Skip-gram (Mikolov et al., 2013), GloVe (Pennington et al., 2014), Multilingual (Faruqui and Dyer, 2014), Dependency-based (Levy and Goldberg, 2014), and FastText (Bojanowski et al., 2016).

For the embeddings with controlled settings, we used two algorithms: W2V Skip-grams and GloVe. We used three different corpora to train these embeddings: Wikipedia 2013 (Wiki), Gigaword[3] (GW) and OpenSubtitles 2016 (OS). We used a centered window of size 10 and generated vectors with 100 dimensions for all 6 models.

From the experiment detailed in Table 1, it appears that GloVe leads to significantly larger negative correlation compared to other approaches, both on the controlled and pretrained settings. On the controlled setting, we notice that the choice of the corpora doesn't significantly affect the correlation. Even if the correlation seems to be higher with the NT-200 and NT-1200 datasets when using the OpenSubtitles corpus, the Steiger test shows that the difference in correlation when using the other corpora is not significant in most cases. However, the algorithms used do have a significant impact on the correlations. In the future, it would be interesting to look at the impact of various other settings such as the size and position of the window, or the dimension of the word vectors.

It can also noted that the correlations on the lexical decision tasks are higher than on the naming tasks which supports the idea that lexical decision

[2]URLs and descriptions available at https://github.com/JomnTAL/spp-wordsim.

[3]LDC2012T21

	Off-the-shelf embeddings					Embeddings with controlled settings					
	GloVe	W2V	Multilingual	Dependency	FastText	GloVe OS	GloVe Wiki	GloVe GW	W2V OS	W2V Wiki	W2V GW
LDT-200	**25.02**	15.35*	13.88*	5.48*	14.48*	23.61	23.06	**23.91**	17.77*	16.75*	16.86*
LDT-1200	**18.91**	11.21*	11.19*	3.76*	10.75*	17.65	17.88	**18.17**	12.86*	11.64*	11.35*
NT-200	**15.43**	5.70*	6.43*	-1.56*	3.73*	**15.37**	12.52*	13.67†	8.27*	6.30*	7.83*
NT-1200	**12.57**	8.86*	7.58*	4.68*	8.30*	**12.14**	10.36†	11.78	9.42*	9.23*	9.30*

Table 1: Spearman's correlation[4] between the test SPP datasets and word embedding models. Highest results are in bold. Significativity of the figures compared to the best results according to Steiger test is indicated by $^*(pval < 0.01)$ and $^\dagger(pval \in [0.01, 0.05[)$.

	Nb Pairs	LDT-200	LDT-1200	NT-200	NT-1200
WS-353-ALL	16	0.40	-0.30	0.26	-0.51
MTurk-771	26	-0.08	0.23	-0.23	-0.28
MEN-TR-3k	71	0.21	-0.20	0.04	-0.02
SimLex-999	101	-0.03	0.06	0.06	0.02

Table 2: Spearman's correlation between reaction times from the SPP datasets and relationship scores from other datasets (with more than 16 overlapping pairs).

seems to be a task less subject to variability from production of the response (pressing a button vs saying a word). Better correlations at an onset of 200 ms can be explained by the fact that subjects are allowed more time to build an intent, leading to more factors being involved. This also probably means that most word embedding models are better at capturing automatic priming mechanisms.

The second experiment detailed in Table 2 looks at the characteristics of the SPP data in regard to other available datasets. We calculated the correlation between the reaction times in the SPP datasets and the relationship scores in a set of existing datasets, using the pairs of words that are available in the two compared datasets (different pairs are compared for each dataset). We only show the results for datasets that have 16 or more pairs in common with the SPP dataset. The SimVerb dataset had 208 pairs in common but since the words used were only verbs whereas in the SPP dataset the part-of-speech wasn't specified, we couldn't really compare the two datasets. It can be observed that the correlations are low which probably means that evaluating on the SPP data could outline different phenomena than what is already covered by relatedness and similarity oriented datasets. Additional work has to be done to fully understand what factors are taken into account by the SPP data.

5 Discussion

It is not clear what cognitive processes lead to mental representations of words in the brain, and it is not clear how these processes relate to linguistic theories. However, reaction time in the context of semantic priming seems to be a good proxy for modeling word embeddings after cognitive processes. The proposed framework addresses some of the problems with word embedding evaluation exposed in (Faruqui et al., 2016)[5]: (2.1) subjectivity is addressed by looking at unconscious phenomena, (2.2) the lexical decision and naming tasks are very general but they are affected by other cognitive pipelines such as vision, (2.3) we provide standardized splits, and (2.5) the size of the dataset allows for significant differences between algorithms. However, we do not address the problem of low correlation with extrinsic evaluation (2.4), we do not account for frequency effects (2.6) and polysemy (2.7). These aspects are left for future work.

6 Conclusion

This work explores an evaluation target for word embeddings: reaction time in lexical decision and naming tasks from a semantic priming experiment. Experiments show that this setting is dominated by different factors than word relatedness or similarity, and that the choice of algorithm is a stronger predictor of correlation than the choice of training corpora. In future work, we will leverage the non-word data from the lexical decision task in order to evaluate character-based word embeddings.

Acknowledgements Research supported by grants ANR-15-CE23-0003 (DATCHA), ANR-16-CONV-0002 (ILCB), ANR-11-LABX-0036 (BLRI) et ANR-11-IDEX-0001-02 (A*MIDEX).

[4]For readability, correlations have been multiplied by -100

[5]According to their section numbers

References

Eneko Agirre, Enrique Alfonseca, Keith Hall, Jana Kravalova, Marius Paşca, and Aitor Soroa. 2009. A study on similarity and relatedness using distributional and wordnet-based approaches. In *Proceedings of Human Language Technologies: The 2009 Annual Conference of the North American Chapter of the Association for Computational Linguistics*. Association for Computational Linguistics, pages 19–27.

Simon Baker, Roi Reichart, and Anna Korhonen. 2014. An unsupervised model for instance level subcategorization acquisition. In *EMNLP*. Citeseer, pages 278–289.

Piotr Bojanowski, Edouard Grave, Armand Joulin, and Tomas Mikolov. 2016. Enriching word vectors with subword information. *arXiv preprint arXiv:1607.04606* 00025.

Elia Bruni, Gemma Boleda, Marco Baroni, and Nam-Khanh Tran. 2012. Distributional semantics in technicolor. In *Proceedings of the 50th Annual Meeting of the Association for Computational Linguistics: Long Papers-Volume 1*. Association for Computational Linguistics, pages 136–145.

Allyson Ettinger and Tal Linzen. 2016. Evaluating vector space models using human semantic priming results. In *Proceedings of the 1st Workshop on Evaluating Vector Space Representations for NLP*. pages 72–77.

Manaal Faruqui and Chris Dyer. 2014. Improving vector space word representations using multilingual correlation. In *Proc. of EACL*.

Manaal Faruqui, Yulia Tsvetkov, Pushpendre Rastogi, and Chris Dyer. 2016. Problems with evaluation of word embeddings using word similarity tasks. *arXiv preprint arXiv:1605.02276* .

Lev Finkelstein, Evgeniy Gabrilovich, Yossi Matias, Ehud Rivlin, Zach Solan, Gadi Wolfman, and Eytan Ruppin. 2001. Placing search in context: The concept revisited. In *Proceedings of the 10th international conference on World Wide Web*. ACM, pages 406–414.

Daniela Gerz, Ivan Vulić, Felix Hill, Roi Reichart, and Anna Korhonen. 2016. SimVerb-3500: A Large-Scale Evaluation Set of Verb Similarity. In *EMNLP*.

Sahar Ghannay, Benoit Favre, Yannick Esteve, and Nathalie Camelin. 2016. Word embedding evaluation and combination. In *of the Language Resources and Evaluation Conference (LREC 2016), Portoroz (Slovenia)*. pages 23–28.

Guy Halawi, Gideon Dror, Evgeniy Gabrilovich, and Yehuda Koren. 2012. Large-scale learning of word relatedness with constraints. In *Proceedings of the 18th ACM SIGKDD international conference on Knowledge discovery and data mining*. ACM, pages 1406–1414.

Felix Hill, Roi Reichart, and Anna Korhonen. 2016. Simlex-999: Evaluating semantic models with (genuine) similarity estimation. *Computational Linguistics* .

Geoff Hollis and Chris Westbury. 2016. The principals of meaning: Extracting semantic dimensions from co-occurrence models of semantics. *Psychonomic bulletin & review* 23(6):1744–1756.

Keith A Hutchison, David A Balota, James H Neely, Michael J Cortese, Emily R Cohen-Shikora, Chi-Shing Tse, Melvin J Yap, Jesse J Bengson, Dale Niemeyer, and Erin Buchanan. 2013. The semantic priming project. *Behavior Research Methods* 45(4):1099–1114.

Keith A Hutchison, James H Neely, and Jeffrey D Johnson. 2001. With great expectations, can two" wrongs" prime a" right"? *Journal of Experimental Psychology Learning Memory and Cognition* 27(6):1451–1463.

Siwei Lai, Kang Liu, Shizhu He, and Jun Zhao. 2016. How to generate a good word embedding. *IEEE Intelligent Systems* 31(6):5–14.

Omer Levy and Yoav Goldberg. 2014. Dependency-based word embeddings. In *ACL (2)*. Citeseer, pages 302–308.

Omer Levy, Yoav Goldberg, and Israel Ramat-Gan. 2014. Linguistic regularities in sparse and explicit word representations. In *CoNLL*. pages 171–180.

Thang Luong, Richard Socher, and Christopher D Manning. 2013. Better word representations with recursive neural networks for morphology. In *CoNLL*. pages 104–113.

Timothy P McNamara. 2005. *Semantic priming: Perspectives from memory and word recognition*. Psychology Press.

Tomas Mikolov, Kai Chen, Greg Corrado, and Jeffrey Dean. 2013. Efficient estimation of word representations in vector space. *arXiv preprint arXiv:1301.3781* .

George A Miller and Walter G Charles. 1991. Contextual correlates of semantic similarity. *Language and cognitive processes* 6(1):1–28.

Jeffrey Pennington, Richard Socher, and Christopher D Manning. 2014. Glove: Global vectors for word representation. In *EMNLP*. volume 14, pages 1532–1543.

Francisco Pereira, Samuel Gershman, Samuel Ritter, and Matthew Botvinick. 2016. A comparative evaluation of off-the-shelf distributed semantic representations for modelling behavioural data. *Cognitive Neuropsychology* 33(3-4):175–190.

Kira Radinsky, Eugene Agichtein, Evgeniy Gabrilovich, and Shaul Markovitch. 2011. A word at a time: computing word relatedness using temporal semantic analysis. In *Proceedings of the 20th international conference on World wide web*. ACM, pages 337–346.

Yu-Ping Ruan, Zhen-Hua Ling, and Yu Hu. 2016. Exploring semantic representation in brain activity using word embeddings. In *EMNLP*. pages 669–679.

Herbert Rubenstein and John B Goodenough. 1965. Contextual correlates of synonymy. *Communications of the ACM* 8(10):627–633.

Tobias Schnabel, Igor Labutov, David M Mimno, and Thorsten Joachims. 2015. Evaluation methods for unsupervised word embeddings. In *EMNLP*. pages 298–307.

Anders Søgaard. 2016. Evaluating word embeddings with fmri and eye-tracking. *ACL 2016* page 116.

James H. Steiger. 1980. Tests for comparing elements of a correlation matrix. *Psychological bulletin* 87(2):245–251. 02852.

Yulia Tsvetkov, Manaal Faruqui, Wang Ling, Guillaume Lample, and Chris Dyer. 2015. Evaluation of word vector representations by subspace alignment .

Dongqiang Yang and David MW Powers. 2006. *Verb similarity on the taxonomy of WordNet*. Masaryk University.

Playing with Embeddings : Evaluating embeddings for Robot Language Learning through MUD Games

Anmol Gulati[*] and **Kumar Krishna Agrawal**[*]
anmol01gulati@gmail.com, kumarkagrawal@gmail.com
Indian Institute of Technology Kharagpur

Abstract

Acquiring language provides a ubiquitous mode of communication, across humans and robots. To this effect, distributional representations of words based on co-occurrence statistics, have provided significant advancements ranging across machine translation to comprehension. In this paper, we study the suitability of using general purpose word-embeddings for language learning in robots. We propose using text-based games as a proxy to evaluating word embedding on real robots. Based in a risk-reward setting, we review the effectiveness of the embeddings in navigating tasks in fantasy games, as an approximation to their performance on more complex scenarios, like language assisted robot navigation.

1 Introduction

Language provides a natural interface for humans to communicate with robots. With their increasing public presence, from self-driving cars and rescue operations to warehouses, it is imperative to reduce this barrier of communication, by improving language learning in mobile robots. For instance, in search and rescue operations one might want to instruct the agents to "Reach the third floor of the blue building". Given the nature of the tasks, it is essential for the agent to accurately infer its current state and parse natural language instructions to corresponding actions.

In recent years, learning continuous representations of words and symbols have become central to dealing with several key problems in natural language understanding. Usually trained to maximize the likelihood of next utterance, these models effectively learn co-occurrence statistics based on corpora, motivated by the distributional hypothesis (Harris, 1954). This objective function, often organizes objects and actions with *similar* semantic information, to close neighborhoods in the corresponding embedding space. Here, the *similarity between words* is often defined by some metric for *similarity* of the word vectors.

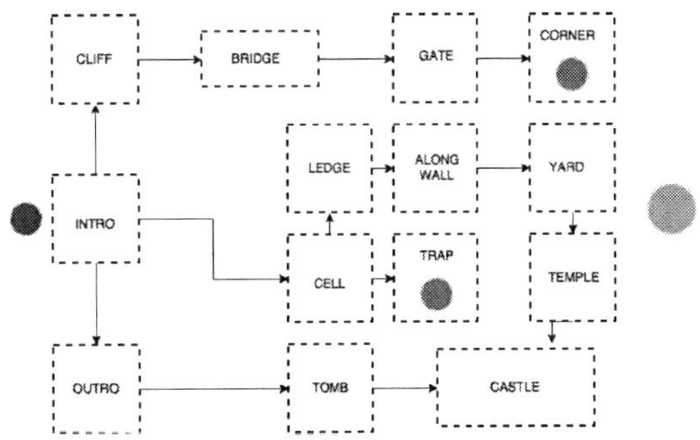

Figure 1: An example of environment generated in the MUD environment. While the blue blob denotes the start state, the red blobs denote deterministic intermediate negative rewards. The green blob on the right denotes positive reward on completion of quest.

Though evidently successful across several tasks, common general purpose word embeddings with fixed dimensions are often inadequate in their representation capacity. In recent works, (Gauthier and Mordatch, 2016; Lucy and Gauthier, 2017) argue that language learning grounded in perception, motion or actions, are important to learn meaningful representations corresponding to *consequences* of actions on objects. Specifically, in a scenario where robots are deployed in real world, it is important to distinguish even between

[*]Equally contributed to the project. Author names listed in alphabetical order.

Proceedings of the 2nd Workshop on Evaluating Vector-Space Representations for NLP, pages 27–30,
Copenhagen, Denmark, September 7–11, 2017. ©2017 Association for Computational Linguistics

Fantasy Environment You are standing very close to the bridges eastern foundation. If you go east you will be back on solid ground ... The bridge sways in the wind.
MARCO dataset (Chen and Mooney, 2011) face the octagon carpet. move until you see red brick floor to your right. turn and walk down the red brick until you get to an alley with grey floor. you should be two alleys away from a lamp and then an easel beyond that.

Table 1: Examples of instructions from MUD vs MARCO dataset for navigation.

similar actions based context and their effect in a given situation.

In this paper, we address this task of evaluating word embeddings for language learning in robots by introducing text-based MUD games (Curtis, 1992) as a proxy. Traditionally in robotics, elaborate simulators have been used to evaluate motor control policies of motion planning for the physical agents. In a similar spirit, MUD games provide a rich playground for define complex scenarios solely with textual descriptions. Based on these, the agents are required to take certain actions with the objective of clearing the quest. (Fig. 1)

To evaluate, we train a LSTM-DQN following (Narasimhan et al., 2015), in a reinforcement learning framework. The agent is trained to learn control policies, with the objective of maximizing the rewards obtained. We demonstrate that using general purpose embeddings improve on the average rewards per quest.

2 Multi-User Dungeon Games

A Multi-User Dungeon Game, as defined in (Curtis, 1992) *"is a network-accessible, multi-participant, user-extensible virtual reality whose user interface is entirely textual"*. In essence, it describes an elaborate environment with multiple characters and tasks for the player, the only constraint being that all interactions with the game are purely textual.

In (Amir and Doyle, 2002), the authors elaborately elucidate the richness of such environments, with insights specific to robotics. Primarily in our context of robot language learning, we make the following observations :

- The environment is partially observable, with stochasticity depending on the actions taken by the agent. This inherently allows us to cast the problem as an MDP, and studying it in the light of recent advances in Deep Reinforcement Learning.
- Intermediate rewards provide feedback to the agent, as proxy for a human in a real-life setting. This allows the agent to learn from consequences and formulating the problem in a risk-reward setting.
- Language based symbolic interface for interaction with the environment. Since language remains consistent across simulator and real world, we assume that the text-world is an accurate replica of the real environment.

Among others, the above characteristics suggest that MUD games provide an ideal sandbox for evaluating word-embeddings for robot language learning.

3 Dataset

We propose using text-based MUD games as proxy for evaluating language learning in robotics. As illustrated in (Table 1) the nature of instructions generated by the game environment are quite similar when compared to real datasets, in this case (Chen and Mooney, 2011).

In this work, we use the Evennia[1]game environment, an open-source library to build online textual MUD games. Evennia allows users to create complex environments with elaborate textural descriptions, by simply writing a batch file to describe the objects, actions and possible interactions in the environment. Compared to other available datasets for navigation, the MUD environment provides a risk-reward scenario, where the environment can also be designed to have deterministic negative feedback to represent undesirable outcomes.

To provide feedback on the action taken, the agents are provided positive/negative rewards depending on the state of the game. In case of quest completion, the agents are provided a large positive reward, while predefined bad intermediate checkpoints like colliding with walls, or falling off bridges are penalized with negative rewards. Building on extensive literature in reward shaping in the Deep Reinforcement Learning framework,

[1]`http://www.evennia.com/`

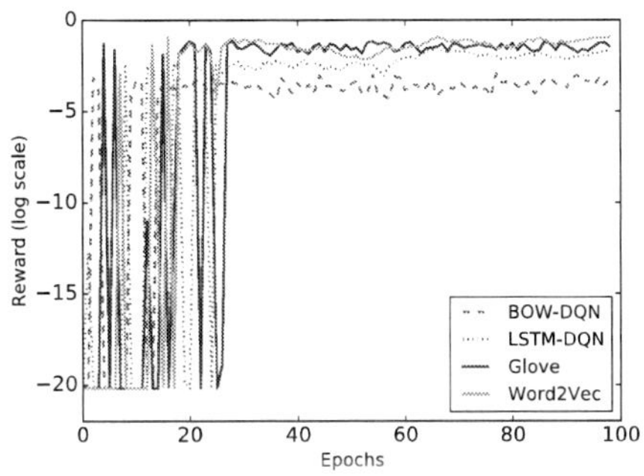

Figure 2: Evaluating agents trained across various embeddings based on average reward (log scale). Pretrained word-vectors outperform random initialized LSTM-DQN and BOW-DQN.

more complex environment can also be easily constructed to evaluate the generalizing capability of the embeddings.

4 Model Architecture

Formulating the problem in a reinforcement learning setting, we train the agent to learn a good Q-value function $Q(s, a)$, for all possible state-action pairs. More concretely the agent iteratively optimizes the Bellman objective

$$Q_{i+1}(s, a) = E[r + \gamma \max_{a'} Q_i(s', a')|s, a] \quad (1)$$

where, γ is the discount factor. With the changing distribution on Q-values the agent decides action a to maximize the future rewards.

In this regard, we follow the LSTM-DQN model by (Narasimhan et al., 2015) which builds on recent developments in Deep Q-Learning (Mnih et al., 2015).

4.1 LSTM-DQN

The input to the agent is the textual description of the current state of the environment. However, the model is required to keep a track over previous states, as well generate a compact representation for the same. Therefore we define a representation generator (ϕ_R), which is an LSTM module to keep a track of the current state of the environment. The individual time step rollouts are further aggregated (ϕ_A) to convert the textual description into compact vector representation (s).

Following the context, the model is required to choose an $action(a)$ to be taken, and an $object(o)$ on which the action is applied in the MUD environment. As a result, we define two Q-value functions $Q(s, a)$ and $Q(s, o)$, which share the same state, and generate distributions on actions and objects respectively. This (a, o) tuple, together defines the action executed by the game environment to update it's state. For detailed description of the model please refer (Narasimhan et al., 2015).

5 Evaluation

We experiment on the *Fantasy World* following the environment in (Narasimhan et al., 2015). The vocabulary consists of 1340 unique tokens, with 100 different descriptions for the room. Visiting the room provides random sequence of description as developed by the designers. Average length of descriptions in the rooms was 65 words per descriptions. The possible actions per state average to 222 per state. Please refer (Narasimhan et al., 2015) for elaborate game statistics.

To evaluate the performance of agents when using different word-embeddings, different metrics could be defined depending on the requirement of the task. In the particular case of evaluating the performance of the agent on navigation task, we follow common defined metrics as in (Narasimhan et al., 2015)

- cumulative reward per episode averaged over the number of episodes.
- fraction of quests successfully completed by the agent.

Considering the task as an downstream proxy for the actual environment, this does not evaluate the individual embeddings by similarity metrics, rather the generalization across environments. In this work we compare word2vec (Mikolov et al., 2013), GloVe (Pennington et al., 2014) general use embeddings against a BOW-DQN baseline and LSTM-DQN trained with random initialization (Fig 2). The baseline here (BOW-DQN) uses a simple bag-of-words model to represent the textual description.

We observe that using pre-trained embeddings generally improve the performance of the model. The rewards in our primary models have high variance due to the stochastic nature of the policy. In further work, we wish to build on recent advancements in Deep Reinforcement Learning literature, for training better models.

6 Discussion and Future Work

Using continuous vector representations of words for language learning in mobile robots poses the question of choice of embeddings which capture task specific semantics. In this work we propose using MUD games as proxy for this task, rather than elaborate testing on robotic platforms.

Similar to real world situation, all interactions between the agent and the environment are through language, without any other supervision. The rewards provide the models with required supervision of tuning the word embeddings to complete the quest. Preliminary evaluation on standard embeddings show that average rewards for pretrained embeddings are better than BOW models and randomly initialized LSTM embeddings.

In future work we wish to extensively evaluate the model on more standard word-embeddings and against real datasets to establish empirical correlation between the proposed proxy and actual task.

References

Eyal Amir and Patrick Doyle. 2002. Adventure games: A challenge for cognitive robotics. pages 148–155.

David L. Chen and Raymond J. Mooney. 2011. Learning to interpret natural language navigation instructions fro mobservations. In *Proceedings of the 25th AAAI Conference on Artificial Intelligence (AAAI-2011)*. San Francisco, CA, USA.

Pavel Curtis. 1992. Mudding: Social phenomena in text-based virtual realities. *High noon on the electronic frontier: Conceptual issues in cyberspace* pages 347–374.

Jon Gauthier and Igor Mordatch. 2016. A paradigm for situated and goal-driven language learning. *arXiv preprint arXiv:1610.03585* .

Zellig S Harris. 1954. Distributional structure. *Word* 10(2-3):146–162.

L. Lucy and J. Gauthier. 2017. Are distributional representations ready for the real world? Evaluating word vectors for grounded perceptual meaning. *ArXiv e-prints* .

Tomas Mikolov, Ilya Sutskever, Kai Chen, Greg S Corrado, and Jeff Dean. 2013. Distributed representations of words and phrases and their compositionality. In *Advances in neural information processing systems*. pages 3111–3119.

Volodymyr Mnih, Koray Kavukcuoglu, David Silver, Andrei A Rusu, Joel Veness, Marc G Bellemare, Alex Graves, Martin Riedmiller, Andreas K Fidjeland, Georg Ostrovski, et al. 2015. Human-level control through deep reinforcement learning. *Nature* 518(7540):529–533.

Karthik Narasimhan, Tejas Kulkarni, and Regina Barzilay. 2015. Language understanding for text-based games using deep reinforcement learning. *arXiv preprint arXiv:1506.08941* .

Jeffrey Pennington, Richard Socher, and Christopher D Manning. 2014. Glove: Global vectors for word representation.

Recognizing Textual Entailment in Twitter Using Word Embeddings

Octavia-Maria Şulea
Human Language Technologies Research Center,
Faculty of Mathematics and Computer Science, University of Bucharest,
Academiei 14, 010014, Bucharest
mary.octavia@gmail.com

Abstract

In this paper, we investigate the application of machine learning techniques and word embeddings to the task of Recognizing Textual Entailment (RTE) in Social Media. We look at a manually labeled dataset (Lendvai et al., 2016) consisting of user generated short texts posted on Twitter (tweets) and related to four recent media events (the Charlie Hebdo shooting, the Ottawa shooting, the Sydney Siege, and the German Wings crash) and test to what extent neural techniques and embeddings are able to distinguish between tweets that entail or contradict each other or that claim unrelated things. We obtain comparable results to the state of the art in a train-test setting, but we show that, due to the noisy aspect of the data, results plummet in an evaluation strategy crafted to better simulate a real-life train-test scenario.

1 Introduction

The ability to automatically deduce how the meaning of text flows from one sentence to the next is a central part of Natural Language Understanding (NLU) and highly important in many Natural Language Processing tasks (NLP). Recognizing Textual Entailment (RTE), started as a challenge in 2004 from this very need and reaching its 8th iteration in 2013 at SemEval[1], falls at the intersection between NLU, NLP, Information Extraction, and Information Retrieval (Dagan et al., 2006). Its goal is, given a pair of sentences dubbed *text* and *hypothesis*, to determine whether the meaning of either (traditionally, of the hypothesis) entails the meaning of the other, contradicts it, or whether nothing can be said of the relationship between the two sentences. Here, the notion of entailment and contradiction are not necessarily related to the linguistic notions, where entailment is always explained in contrast with presupposition and sometimes implicature(Sauerland, 2007), but are outlined in (de Marneffe et al., 2008).

Interest in this task was amplified with the creation of the SNLI corpus (Bowman et al., 2015) which lead to a few studies using Deep Neural Networks (DNN) (Wang and Jiang, 2016; Rocktäschel et al., 2015). Previous to this, the Excitement Open Platform [2] was considered the state-of-the-art model.

On the hand, interest in ways to represent text in order to improve performance in text classification (Lilleberg et al., 2015; Joulin et al., 2016), machine translation (Zou et al., 2013; Sulea et al., 2016) or question answering tasks (Sharp et al., 2016) has been rekindled with the introduction of the highly cited word2vec model (Mikolov et al., 2013) and the avenue of deep neural word embeddings (Palangi et al., 2016).

Our present research revolved around three questions:

- Can we apply state of the art neural methods created for large datasets or longer texts to small datasets containing very short texts?
- Will these methods work for fine grained contradictions?
- Can word embeddings, which were successfully used for word-level semantic tasks, improve performance in tasks pertaining to discourse level semantics?

[1] https://www.cs.york.ac.uk/semeval-2013/task7/

[2] http://hltfbk.github.io/Excitement-Open-Platform/

Proceedings of the 2nd Workshop on Evaluating Vector-Space Representations for NLP, pages 31–35,
Copenhagen, Denmark, September 7–11, 2017. ©2017 Association for Computational Linguistics

2 Approach

In this paper we investigate the application of several state-of-the art approaches to the RTE task in the social media domain and investigate the use of word embeddings for what is essentially a discourse level semantic task. We use neural networks and compare our results with the results obtained previously using classical "feature engineering" methods.

2.1 Data

The data we used was presented in (Lendvai et al., 2016). It contains around 5000 Tweet pairs, distributed over four recent media events, reported in the press. These pairs were hand labeled as being either in a relationship of *entailment*, meaning that the underlying sense of each of the two text snippets was effectively the same, a relationship of *contradiction*, meaning that information in one of the tweets as minor as the number of victims or location of the event at hand contradicted the information expressed in the other tweet, or the two tweets were labeled to be in an *unknown* relationship, meaning that their underlying *stories* did not entail nor contradict each other, although they were referring to the same event. The dataset was slightly unbalanced, with the majority class pertaining to that of the *unknown* relationship and the minority class to the *contradiction* relationship.

Since the contradiction manifested between tweet pairs labeled was very fine grained, we expected bag of word models to perform poorly and confusion between entailment and contradiction to be high. Also, since, for each event, all three classes were represented, there was an expectation that BOW and similarity measures based on BOW would also fail, since pairs of tweets talking about the same event, but being in completely different relationships were abundant. Indeed, as can be seen from the results reported in (Lendvai et al., 2016), the f1 measure is slightly above the random baseline when using such features.

2.2 Classifier Implementation and Settings

For the implementation of the Multi Layer Perceptron classifier, we used the python library Keras [3] which wraps over the Deep Learning library for Python, Theano (Theano Development Team, 2016). The pre-trained word2vec model offered by Google was loaded into our system using the Gensim library (Řehůřek and Sojka, 2010). For the word-mover distance, we used pyemd [4], a Python wrapper for Pele and Werman's implementation of the Earth Mover's Distance metric (Pele and Werman, 2008).

The neural network was trained using several settings for the hyper-parameters (batch size and number of epochs) and we report the results for a batch size of 50 over 100 epochs. We also investigated several ways of representing the *t* and *h* text pairs.

2.3 Feature Representation

The first choice in representing the sentence pairs was to sum the 300-sized vector representation for each word in each of the two sentences separately and then concatenate the resulting 300-sized vectors into one. This lead to one 600-sized vectorial representation of the sentence pair. The second strategy lead to a 900-sized vector: the first 300 elements represented the sum of the vectors of words in the *t* text, the following 300 elements were 0s representing the separation vector, and the final 300 positions in the vector represented the sum of the vector for each word in the *h* text.

We also applied different similarity measures, including cosine and word mover's distance (Kusner et al., 2015), over the vectorial representations of the tweets. Ultimately, in terms of feature representation, we wanted to test two things:

- whether distance metrics between vectorial representations (weather one-hot or word2vec) of tweets are sufficient in predicting the RTE class
- whether inserting a *separation vector* between the two vectors for each of the texts in the pair leads to better results.

2.4 Event-based Cross Validation

In order to have a testing setup as close to a real-life scenario as possible, we employed the event-based cross validation, as proposed in (Lendvai et al., 2016). This effectively meant that, for each of the four events, we kept the tweets related to the other three events for training and used the tweets from the fourth event for testing. This meant that we had a 4-fold cross validation, where, for each *fold*, the train-test split was based on the event

[3] https://keras.io

[4] https://github.com/wmayner/pyemd

each pair belonged to. This in turn meant that, although the event label was never directly used as a feature or as the predicted label, it was indirectly used in cross-validation. This strategy was employed to simulate a real-life scenario where the end user of such an RTE system (e.g. a journalist trying to make sense of a large set of tweets on one event), would already have at their disposal a classification model pre-trained on other, possibly unrelated, events. We compared the results of event based cross-validation with typical train-test split results.

3 Results

Table 1 show the event-based cross validation results for the 3-way classification task when the features used are cosine distance between the sum of word2vec representation of the words in each tweet and word mover distance. More precisely, the cosine value and the word-mover distance value were concatenated to form a Nx2 feature matrix, where N was the number of input examples.

Model	Method	P	R	F
SVM	avg.	0.45	0.52	0.45
LR	avg.	0.46	0.52	0.45
Base	avg.	0.33	0.33	0.33
SVM	cont	0.38	0.49	0.40
LR	cont	0.43	0.53	0.46
Base	cont	0.26	0.31	0.28

Table 1: Event-based CV results using cosine similarity and word mover distance on the minority class and averaged

As can be seen from Figure 1, the distance metrics on occurrence vectors and word2vec summation vector are not good features to separate the three classes.

Logistic regression performed similar to Linear SVC when applied to the word2vec representation coupled with the word mover distance and averaging the event-based cross-validation results over all three classes. However, for the minority class contradiction, LR seemed to perform slightly better, although the standard deviation computed over each fold was higher.

For the 600 and 900 dimensional vector representation, the event-based CV results were slightly lower, as can be seen from Table 2.

Model	Method	P	R	F
MLP	avg.	0.41	0.34	0.30
LR	avg.	0.42	0.47	0.41
Dummy	avg.	0.35	0.35	0.35

Table 2: Event Based CV results for 900 dimensional vectors

Table 3 shows the train-test split results for the MLP and LR models over 900 dimensional vector

Model	Method	P	R	F
MLP	avg.	0.91	0.90	0.90
LR	avg.	0.78	0.78	0.78
Dummy	avg.	0.33	0.33	0.33
MLP	cont	0.87	0.77	0.82
LR	cont	0.62	0.60	0.61
Dummy	cont	0.26	0.26	0.26

Table 3: Train-Test Split results for LSTM and Logistic Regression

4 Conclusions and Future Work

In this paper we've investigated the use of current day classification tools for the task of recognizing textual entailment in Twitter data. We've shown that the same neural network models successfully used in the same task but on larger datasets perform similarly well (with only a small drop in performance) in a train-test split evaluation setting, but they perform as poorly as any other classifier in the event-based cross validation setting, a novel evaluation strategy, which was previously proposed to better simulate real life scenarios of RTE systems on Twitter.

We've also seen that using only the distance (co sine, word mover) between vector representations of the tweets, be those bow or sum of word2vec, was not enough to distinguish the minority class in the event-based cross validation setting and that using concatenation of word2vec leads to minor improvements in the same setting, but considerable in the train-test one.

Acknowledgements

Work presented in this paper has been supported by the PHEME FP7 project (grant No. 611233).

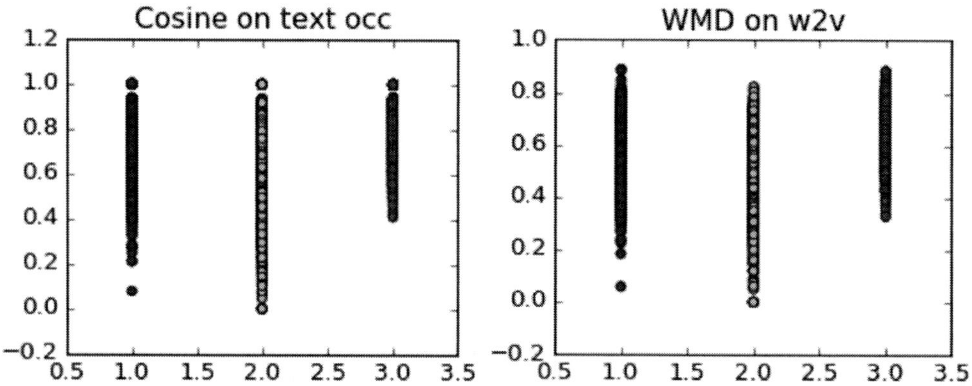

Figure 1: Plot of cosine distance on occurrence vector representation and word mover distance on word2vec summation representation for h and t; the horizontal axis represents the three classes and the vertical represents the distance values

References

Samuel R. Bowman, Gabor Angeli, Christopher Potts, and Christopher D. Manning. 2015. A large annotated corpus for learning natural language inference. In Lluís Màrquez, Chris Callison-Burch, Jian Su, Daniele Pighin, and Yuval Marton, editors, *Proceedings of the 2015 Conference on Empirical Methods in Natural Language Processing, EMNLP 2015, Lisbon, Portugal, September 17-21, 2015*. The Association for Computational Linguistics, pages 632–642. http://aclweb.org/anthology/D/D15/D151075.pdf.

Ido Dagan, Oren Glickman, and Bernardo Magnini. 2006. The pascal recognising textual entailment challenge. In *Proceedings of the First International Conference on Machine Learning Challenges: Evaluating Predictive Uncertainty Visual Object Classification, and Recognizing Textual Entailment*. Springer-Verlag, Berlin, Heidelberg, MLCW'05, pages 177–190.

Marie-Catherine de Marneffe, Anna N. Rafferty, and Christopher D. Manning. 2008. Finding contradictions in text. In Kathleen McKeown, Johanna D. Moore, Simone Teufel, James Allan, and Sadaoki Furui, editors, *ACL 2008, Proceedings of the 46th Annual Meeting of the Association for Computational Linguistics, June 15-20, 2008, Columbus, Ohio, USA*. The Association for Computer Linguistics, pages 1039–1047. http://www.aclweb.org/anthology/P08-1118.

Armand Joulin, Edouard Grave, Piotr Bojanowski, Matthijs Douze, Hervé Jégou, and Tomas Mikolov. 2016. Fasttext.zip: Compressing text classification models. *CoRR* abs/1612.03651. http://arxiv.org/abs/1612.03651.

Matt J. Kusner, Yu Sun, Nicholas I. Kolkin, and Kilian Q. Weinberger. 2015. From word embeddings to document distances. In Francis R. Bach and David M. Blei, editors, *Proceedings of the 32nd International Conference on Machine Learning, ICML 2015, Lille, France, 6-11 July 2015*. JMLR.org, volume 37 of *JMLR Workshop and Conference Proceedings*, pages 957–966. http://jmlr.org/proceedings/papers/v37/kusnerb15.html.

Piroska Lendvai, Isabelle Augenstein, Kalina Bontcheva, and Thierry Declerck. 2016. Monolingual social media datasets for detecting contradiction and entailment. In Nicoletta Calzolari (Conference Chair), Khalid Choukri (Conference Chair), Thierry Declerck, Sara Goggi, Marko Grobelnik, Bente Maegaard, Joseph Mariani, Hlne Mazo, Asuncion Moreno, Jan Odijk, and Stelios Piperidis, editors, *Proceedings of the Tenth International Conference on Language Resources and Evaluation (LREC'16)*. ELRA, ELRA, 9, rue des Cordelires, 75013 Paris, 5/2016.

Joseph Lilleberg, Yun Zhu, and Yanqing Zhang. 2015. Support vector machines and word2vec for text classification with semantic features. In Ning Ge, Jianhua Lu, Yingxu Wang, Newton Howard, Philip Chen, Xiaoming Tao, Bo Zhang, and Lotfi A. Zadeh, editors, *14th IEEE International Conference on Cognitive Informatics & Cognitive Computing, ICCI*CC 2015, Beijing, China, July 6-8, 2015*. IEEE Computer Society, pages 136–140. https://doi.org/10.1109/ICCI-CC.2015.7259377.

Tomas Mikolov, Ilya Sutskever, Kai Chen, Gregory S. Corrado, and Jeffrey Dean. 2013. Distributed representations of words and phrases and their compositionality. In Christopher J. C. Burges, Léon Bottou, Zoubin Ghahramani, and Kilian Q. Weinberger, editors, *Advances in Neural Information Processing Systems 26: 27th Annual Conference on Neural Information Processing Systems 2013. Proceedings of a meeting held December 5-8, 2013, Lake Tahoe, Nevada, United States.*. pages

3111–3119. http://papers.nips.cc/paper/5021-distributed-representations-of-words-and-phrases-and-their-compositionality.

Hamid Palangi, Li Deng, Yelong Shen, Jianfeng Gao, Xiaodong He, Jianshu Chen, Xinying Song, and Rabab K. Ward. 2016. Deep sentence embedding using long short-term memory networks: Analysis and application to information retrieval. *IEEE/ACM Trans. Audio, Speech & Language Processing* 24(4):694–707. https://doi.org/10.1109/TASLP.2016.2520371.

Ofir Pele and Michael Werman. 2008. A linear time histogram metric for improved sift matching. In *Computer Vision–ECCV 2008*. Springer, pages 495–508.

Radim Řehůřek and Petr Sojka. 2010. Software Framework for Topic Modelling with Large Corpora. In *Proceedings of the LREC 2010 Workshop on New Challenges for NLP Frameworks*. ELRA, Valletta, Malta, pages 45–50. http://is.muni.cz/publication/884893/en.

Tim Rocktäschel, Edward Grefenstette, Karl Moritz Hermann, Tomás Kociský, and Phil Blunsom. 2015. Reasoning about entailment with neural attention. *CoRR* abs/1509.06664. http://arxiv.org/abs/1509.06664.

U Sauerland. 2007. *Presupposition and Implicature in Compositional Semantics*.

Rebecca Sharp, Mihai Surdeanu, Peter Jansen, Peter Clark, and Michael Hammond. 2016. Creating causal embeddings for question answering with minimal supervision. *CoRR* abs/1609.08097. http://arxiv.org/abs/1609.08097.

Octavia-Maria Sulea, Sergiu Nisioi, and Liviu P. Dinu. 2016. Using word embeddings to translate named entities. In Nicoletta Calzolari, Khalid Choukri, Thierry Declerck, Sara Goggi, Marko Grobelnik, Bente Maegaard, Joseph Mariani, Hélène Mazo, Asunción Moreno, Jan Odijk, and Stelios Piperidis, editors, *Proceedings of the Tenth International Conference on Language Resources and Evaluation LREC 2016, Portorož, Slovenia, May 23-28, 2016.*. European Language Resources Association (ELRA). http://www.lrec-conf.org/proceedings/lrec2016/summaries/1167.html.

Theano Development Team. 2016. Theano: A Python framework for fast computation of mathematical expressions. *arXiv e-prints* abs/1605.02688. http://arxiv.org/abs/1605.02688.

Shuohang Wang and Jing Jiang. 2016. Learning natural language inference with LSTM. In Kevin Knight, Ani Nenkova, and Owen Rambow, editors, *NAACL HLT 2016, The 2016 Conference of the North American Chapter of the Association for Computational Linguistics: Human Language Technologies, San Diego California, USA, June 12-17, 2016*. The Association for Computational Linguistics, pages 1442–1451. http://aclweb.org/anthology/N/N16/N16-1170.pdf.

Will Y. Zou, Richard Socher, Daniel M. Cer, and Christopher D. Manning. 2013. Bilingual word embeddings for phrase-based machine translation. In *Proceedings of the 2013 Conference on Empirical Methods in Natural Language Processing, EMNLP 2013, 18-21 October 2013, Grand Hyatt Seattle, Seattle, Washington, USA, A meeting of SIGDAT, a Special Interest Group of the ACL*. ACL, pages 1393–1398. http://aclweb.org/anthology/D/D13/D13-1141.pdf.

Recurrent Neural Network-Based Sentence Encoder with Gated Attention for Natural Language Inference

Qian Chen
University of Science and Technology of China
cq1231@mail.ustc.edu.cn

Xiaodan Zhu
Queen's University
xiaodan.zhu@queensu.ca

Zhen-Hua Ling
University of Science and Technology of China
zhling@ustc.edu.cn

Si Wei
iFLYTEK Research
siwei@iflytek.com

Hui Jiang
York University
hj@cse.yorku.ca

Diana Inkpen
University of Ottawa
diana@site.uottawa.ca

Abstract

The RepEval 2017 Shared Task aims to evaluate natural language understanding models for sentence representation, in which a sentence is represented as a fixed-length vector with neural networks and the quality of the representation is tested with a natural language inference task. This paper describes our system (alpha) that is ranked among the top in the Shared Task, on both the in-domain test set (obtaining a 74.9% accuracy) and on the cross-domain test set (also attaining a 74.9% accuracy), demonstrating that the model generalizes well to the cross-domain data. Our model is equipped with intra-sentence gated-attention composition which helps achieve a better performance. In addition to submitting our model to the Shared Task, we have also tested it on the Stanford Natural Language Inference (SNLI) dataset. We obtain an accuracy of 85.5%, which is the best reported result on SNLI when cross-sentence attention is not allowed, the same condition enforced in RepEval 2017.

1 Introduction

The RepEval 2017 Shared Task aims to evaluate language understanding models for sentence representation with natural language inference (NLI) tasks, where a sentence is represented as a fixed-length vector.

Modeling inference in human language is very challenging but is a basic problem in natural language understanding. Specifically, NLI is concerned with determining whether a hypothesis sentence h can be inferred from a premise sentence p.

Most previous top-performing neural network models on NLI use attention models between a premise and its hypothesis, while how much information can be encoded in a fixed-length vector without such cross-sentence attention deserves some further understanding. In this paper, we describe the model we submitted to the RepEval 2017 Shared Task (Nangia et al., 2017), which achieves the top performance on both the in-domain and cross-domain test set.

2 Related Work

Natural language inference (NLI), also named recognizing textual entailment (RTE) includes a large bulk of early work on rather small datasets with more conventional methods (Dagan et al., 2005; MacCartney, 2009). More recently, the large datasets are available, which makes it possible to train natural language inference models based on neural networks (Bowman et al., 2015; Williams et al., 2017).

Natural language inference models based on neural networks are mainly separated into two kind of ways, sentence encoder-based models and cross-sentence attention-based models. Among them, Enhanced Sequential Inference Model (ESIM) with cross-sentence attention represents the state of the art (Chen et al., 2016b). However, in this paper we principally concentrate on

Proceedings of the 2nd Workshop on Evaluating Vector-Space Representations for NLP, pages 36–40,
Copenhagen, Denmark, September 7–11, 2017. ©2017 Association for Computational Linguistics

sentence encoder-based model. Many researchers have studied sentence encoder-based model for natural language inference (Bowman et al., 2015; Vendrov et al., 2015; Mou et al., 2016; Bowman et al., 2016; Munkhdalai and Yu, 2016a,b; Liu et al., 2016; Lin et al., 2017). It is, however, not very clear if the potential of the sentence encoder-based model has been well exploited. In this paper, we demonstrate that proposed models based on gated-attention can achieve a new state-of-the-art performance for natural language inference.

3 Methods

We present here the proposed natural language inference networks which are composed of the following major components: word embedding, sequence encoder, composition layer, and the top-layer classifier. Figure 1 shows a view of the architecture of our neural language inference network.

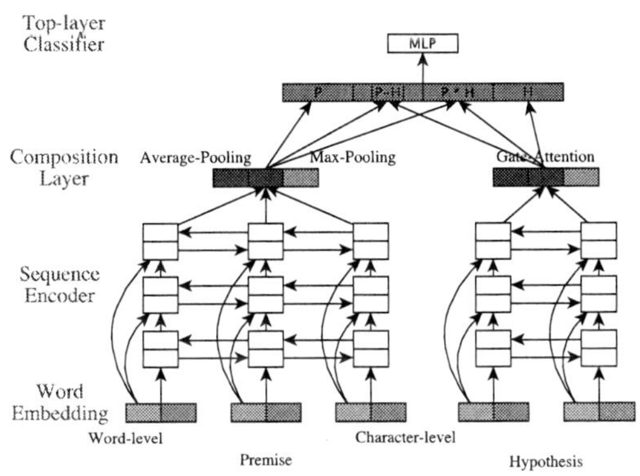

Figure 1: A view of our neural language inference network.

3.1 Word Embedding

In our notation, a sentence (premise or hypothesis) is indicated as $x = (x_1, \dots, x_l)$, where l is the length of the sentence. We concatenate embeddings learned at two different levels to represent each word in the sentence: the character composition and holistic word-level embedding. The character composition feeds all characters of each word into a convolutional neural network (CNN) with max-pooling (Kim, 2014) to obtain representations $c = (c_1, \dots, c_l)$. In addition, we also use the pre-trained GloVe vectors (Pennington et al., 2014) for each word as holistic word-level embedding $w = (w_1, \dots, w_l)$. Therefore, each word is represented as a concatenation of the character-composition vector and word-level embedding $e = ([c_1; w_1], \dots, [c_l; w_l])$. This is performed on both the premise and hypothesis, resulting into two matrices: the $e^p \in \mathbb{R}^{n \times d_w}$ for a premise and the $e^h \in \mathbb{R}^{m \times d_w}$ for a hypothesis, where n and m are the length of the premise and hypothesis respectively, and d_w is the embedding dimension.

3.2 Sequence Encoder

To represent words and their context in a premise and hypothesis, sentence pairs are fed into sentence encoders to obtain hidden vectors (h^p and h^h). We use stacked bidirectional LSTMs (BiLSTM) as the encoders. Shortcut connections are applied, which concatenate word embeddings and input hidden states at each layer in the stacked BiLSTM except for the bottom layer.

$$h^p = \text{BiLSTM}(e^p) \in \mathbb{R}^{n \times 2d} \quad (1)$$

$$h^h = \text{BiLSTM}(e^h) \in \mathbb{R}^{m \times 2d} \quad (2)$$

where d is the dimension of hidden states of LSTMs. A BiLSTM concatenate a forward and backward LSTM on a sequence $h_t = [\overrightarrow{h_t}; \overleftarrow{h_t}]$, starting from the left and the right end, respectively. Hidden states of unidirectional LSTM ($\overrightarrow{h_t}$ or $\overleftarrow{h_t}$) are calculated as follows,

$$\begin{bmatrix} i_t \\ f_t \\ u_t \\ o_t \end{bmatrix} = \begin{bmatrix} \sigma \\ \sigma \\ \tanh \\ \sigma \end{bmatrix} (W x_t + U h_{t-1} + b) \quad (3)$$

$$c_t = f_t \odot c_{t-1} + i_t \odot u_t \quad (4)$$

$$h_t = o_t \odot \tanh(c_t) \quad (5)$$

where σ is the sigmoid function, $\odot$ is the element-wise multiplication of two vectors, and $W \in \mathbb{R}^{4d \times d_w}$, $U \in \mathbb{R}^{4d \times d}$, $b \in \mathbb{R}^{4d \times 1}$ are weight matrices to be learned. For each input vector x_t at time step t, LSTM applies a set of gating functions—the input gate i_t, forget gate f_t, and output gate o_t, together with a memory cell c_t, to control message flow and track long-distance information (Hochreiter and Schmidhuber, 1997) and generate a hidden state h_t at each time step.

3.3 Composition Layer

To transform sentences into fixed-length vector representations and reason using those representations, we need to compose the hidden vectors obtained by the sequence encoder layer (h^p and h^h).

We propose intra-sentence gated-attention to obtain a fixed-length vector. Illustrated by the case of hidden states of premise h^p,

$$v_g^p = \sum_{t=1}^{n} \frac{\|i_t\|_2}{\sum_{j=1}^{n} \|i_j\|_2} h_t^p \tag{6}$$

$$\text{or } v_g^p = \sum_{t=1}^{n} \frac{\|1 - f_t\|_2}{\sum_{j=1}^{n} \|1 - f_j\|_2} h_t^p \tag{7}$$

$$\text{or } v_g^p = \sum_{t=1}^{n} \frac{\|o_t\|_2}{\sum_{j=1}^{n} \|o_j\|_2} h_t^p \tag{8}$$

where i_t, f_t, o_t are the input gate, forget gate, and output gate in the BiLSTM of the top layer. Note that the gates are concatenated by forward and backward LSTM, i.e., $i_t = [\overrightarrow{i_t}; \overleftarrow{i_t}]$, $f_t = [\overrightarrow{f_t}; \overleftarrow{f_t}]$, $o_t = [\overrightarrow{o_t}; \overleftarrow{o_t}]$. $\|*\|_2$ indicates l^2-norm, which converts vectors to scalars. The idea of gated-attention is inspired by the fact that human only remember important parts after they read sentences. (Liu et al., 2016; Lin et al., 2017) proposed a similar "inner-attention" mechanism but it's calculated by an extra MLP layer which would require more computation than us.

We also use average-pooling and max-pooling to obtain fixed-length vectors v_a and v_m as in Chen et al. (2016b). Then, the final fixed-length vector representation of premise is $v^p = [v_g^p; v_a^p; v_m^p]$. As for hidden states of hypothesis h^h, we can obtain v^h through similar calculation procedure. Consequently, both the premise and hypothesis are fed into the composition layer to obtain fixed-length vector representations respectively (v^p, v^h).

3.4 Top-layer Classifier

Our inference model feeds the resulting vectors obtained above to the final classifier to determine the overall inference relationship. In our models, we compute the absolute difference and the element-wise product for the tuple $[v^p, v^h]$. The absolute difference and element-wise product are then concatenated with the original vectors v^p and v^h (Mou et al., 2016).

$$v_{\text{inp}} = [v^p; v^h; |v^p - v^h|; v^p \odot v^h] \tag{9}$$

We then put the vector v_{inp} into a final multi-layer perceptron (MLP) classifier. The MLP has 2 hidden layers with *ReLu* activation with shortcut connections and a *softmax* output layer in our experiments. The entire model (all four components described above) is trained end-to-end, and the cross-entropy loss of the training set is minimized.

4 Experimental Setup

Data RepEval 2017 use Multi-Genre NLI corpus (MultiNLI) (Williams et al., 2017), which focuses on three basic relationships between a premise and a potential hypothesis: the premise entails the hypothesis (*entailment*), they contradict each other (*contradiction*), or they are not related (*neutral*). The corpus has ten genres, such as fiction, letters, telephone speech and so on. Training set only has five genres of them, therefore there are in-domain and cross-domain development/test sets. SNLI (Bowman et al., 2015) corpus can be used as an additional training/development set, which includes content from the single genre of image captions. However, we don't use SNLI as an additional training/development data in our experiments.

Training We use the in-domain development set to select models for testing. To help replicate our results, we publish our code at `https://github.com/lukecq1231/enc_nli` (the core code is also used or adapted for a summarization (Chen et al., 2016a) and a question-answering task (Zhang et al., 2017)). We use the Adam (Kingma and Ba, 2014) for optimization. Stacked BiLSTM has 3 layers, and all hidden states of BiLSTMs and MLP have 600 dimensions. The character embedding has 15 dimensions, and CNN filters length is [1,3,5], each of those is 100 dimensions. We use pre-trained *GloVe-840B-300D* vectors (Pennington et al., 2014) as our word-level embeddings and fix these embeddings during the training process. Out-of-vocabulary (OOV) words are initialized randomly with Gaussian samples.

5 Results

Table 1 shows the results of different models. The first group of models are copied from Williams et al. (2017). The first sentence encoder is based on continuous bag of words (CBOW), the second is based on BiLSTM, and the third model is Enhanced Sequential Inference Model (ESIM) (Chen et al., 2016b) reimplemented by Williams et al. (2017), which represents the state of the art on SNLI dataset. However, ESIM uses attention between sentence pairs, which is not a sentence-encoder based model.

Model	In	Cross
CBOW	64.8	64.5
BiLSTM	66.9	66.9
ESIM	72.3	72.1
TALP-UPC*	67.9	68.2
LCT-MALTA*	70.7	70.8
Rivercorners*	72.1	72.1
Rivercorners (ensemble)*	72.2	72.8
YixinNie-UNC-NLP*	74.5	73.5
Our ESIM	76.8	75.8
Single*	73.5	73.6
Ensembled*	74.9	74.9
Single (Input Gate)*	73.5	73.6
Single (Forget Gate)	72.9	73.1
Single (Output Gate)	73.7	73.4
Single - Gated-Att	72.8	73.6
Single - CharCNN	72.9	73.5
Single - Word Embedding	65.6	66.0
Single - AbsDiff/Product	69.7	69.2

Table 1: Accuracies of the models on MultiNLI. Note that * indicates that the model participate in the competition on June 15th, 2017.

The second group of models are the results of other teams which participate the RepEval 2017 Share Task competition (Nangia et al., 2017).

In addition, we also use our implementation of ESIM, which achieves an accuracy of 76.8% in the in-domain test set, and 75.8% in the cross-domain test set, which presents the state-of-the-art results. After removing the cross-sentence attention and adding our gated-attention model, we achieve accuracies of 73.5% and 73.6%, which ranks first in the cross-domain test set and ranks second in the in-domain test set among the single models. When ensembling our models, we obtain accuracies 74.9% and 74.9%, which ranks first in both test sets. Our ensembling is performed by averaging the five models trained with different parameter initialization.

We compare the performance of using different gate in gate-attention in the fourth group of Table 1. Note that we use attention based on input gate on all other experiments.

To understand the importance of the different elements of the proposed model, we remove some crucial elements from our single model. If we remove the gated-attention, the accuracies drop to 72.8% and 73.6%. If we remove character-composition vector, the accuracies drop to 72.9% and 73.5%. If we remove word-level embedding, the accuracies drop to 65.6% and 66.0%. If we remove absolute difference and element-wise product of the sentence representation vectors, the accuracies drop to 69.7% and 69.2%.

Model	Test
LSTM (Bowman et al., 2015)	80.6
GRU (Vendrov et al., 2015)	81.4
Tree CNN (Mou et al., 2016)	82.1
SPINN-PI (Bowman et al., 2016)	83.2
NTI (Munkhdalai and Yu, 2016b)	83.4
Intra-Att BiLSTM (Liu et al., 2016)	84.2
Self-Att BiLSTM (Lin et al., 2017)	84.2
NSE (Munkhdalai and Yu, 2016a)	84.6
Gated-Att BiLSTM	85.5

Table 2: Accuracies of the models on SNLI.

In addition to testing on this shared task, we have also applied our best single system (without ensembling) on the SNLI dataset; our model achieve an accuracy of 85.5%, which is best result reported on SNLI, outperforming all previous models when cross-sentence attention is not allowed. The previous state-of-the-art sentence encoder-based model (Munkhdalai and Yu, 2016b), called neural semantic encoders (NSE), only achieved an accuracy of 84.6% on SNLI. Table 2 shows the results of previous models and proposed model.

6 Summary and Future Work

We describe our system that encodes a sentence to a fixed-length vector for natural language inference, which achieves the top performances on both the RepEval-2017 and the SNLI dataset. The model is equipped with a novel intra-sentence gated-attention component. The model only uses a common stacked BiLSTM as the building block together with the intra-sentence gated-attention in order to compose the fixed-length representations. Our model could be used on other sentence encoding tasks. Future work on NLI includes exploring the usefulness of external resources such as WordNet and contrasting-meaning embedding (Chen et al., 2015).

Acknowledgments

The first and the third author of this paper were supported in part by the National Natural Science Foundation of China (Grants No. U1636201) and the Fundamental Research Funds for the Central Universities (Grant No. WK2350000001).

References

R. Samuel Bowman, Gabor Angeli, Christopher Potts, and D. Christopher Manning. 2015. A large annotated corpus for learning natural language inference. In *Proceedings of the 2015 Conference on Empirical Methods in Natural Language Processing*. Association for Computational Linguistics, pages 632–642. https://doi.org/10.18653/v1/D15-1075.

R. Samuel Bowman, Jon Gauthier, Abhinav Rastogi, Raghav Gupta, D. Christopher Manning, and Christopher Potts. 2016. A fast unified model for parsing and sentence understanding. In *Proceedings of the 54th Annual Meeting of the Association for Computational Linguistics (Volume 1: Long Papers)*. Association for Computational Linguistics, pages 1466–1477. https://doi.org/10.18653/v1/P16-1139.

Qian Chen, Xiaodan Zhu, Zhen-Hua Ling, Si Wei, and Hui Jiang. 2016a. Distraction-based neural networks for modeling document. In Subbarao Kambhampati, editor, *Proceedings of the Twenty-Fifth International Joint Conference on Artificial Intelligence, IJCAI 2016, New York, NY, USA, 9-15 July 2016*. IJCAI/AAAI Press, pages 2754–2760. http://www.ijcai.org/Abstract/16/391.

Qian Chen, Xiaodan Zhu, Zhen-Hua Ling, Si Wei, and Hui Jiang. 2016b. Enhanced LSTM for natural language inference. *CoRR* abs/1609.06038. http://arxiv.org/abs/1609.06038.

Zhigang Chen, Wei Lin, Qian Chen, Xiaoping Chen, Si Wei, Hui Jiang, and Xiaodan Zhu. 2015. Revisiting word embedding for contrasting meaning. In *Proceedings of the 53rd Annual Meeting of the Association for Computational Linguistics and the 7th International Joint Conference on Natural Language Processing (Volume 1: Long Papers)*. Association for Computational Linguistics, pages 106–115. https://doi.org/10.3115/v1/P15-1011.

Ido Dagan, Oren Glickman, and Bernardo Magnini. 2005. The pascal recognising textual entailment challenge. In *MLCW*.

Sepp Hochreiter and Jürgen Schmidhuber. 1997. Long short-term memory. *Neural Computation* 9(8):1735–1780. https://doi.org/10.1162/neco.1997.9.8.1735.

Yoon Kim. 2014. Convolutional neural networks for sentence classification. *arXiv preprint arXiv:1408.5882* .

Diederik P. Kingma and Jimmy Ba. 2014. Adam: A method for stochastic optimization. *CoRR* abs/1412.6980. http://arxiv.org/abs/1412.6980.

Zhouhan Lin, Minwei Feng, Cícero Nogueira dos Santos, Mo Yu, Bing Xiang, Bowen Zhou, and Yoshua Bengio. 2017. A structured self-attentive sentence embedding. *CoRR* abs/1703.03130. http://arxiv.org/abs/1703.03130.

Yang Liu, Chengjie Sun, Lei Lin, and Xiaolong Wang. 2016. Learning natural language inference using bidirectional LSTM model and inner-attention. *CoRR* abs/1605.09090. http://arxiv.org/abs/1605.09090.

Bill MacCartney. 2009. *Natural Language Inference*. Ph.D. thesis, Stanford University.

Lili Mou, Rui Men, Ge Li, Yan Xu, Lu Zhang, Rui Yan, and Zhi Jin. 2016. Natural language inference by tree-based convolution and heuristic matching. In *Proceedings of the 54th Annual Meeting of the Association for Computational Linguistics (Volume 2: Short Papers)*. Association for Computational Linguistics, pages 130–136. https://doi.org/10.18653/v1/P16-2022.

Tsendsuren Munkhdalai and Hong Yu. 2016a. Neural semantic encoders. *CoRR* abs/1607.04315. http://arxiv.org/abs/1607.04315.

Tsendsuren Munkhdalai and Hong Yu. 2016b. Neural tree indexers for text understanding. *CoRR* abs/1607.04492. http://arxiv.org/abs/1607.04492.

Nikita Nangia, Adina Williams, Angeliki Lazaridou, and Samuel R. Bowman. 2017. The repeval 2017 shared task: Multi-genre natural language inference with sentence representations. In *Proceedings of RepEval 2017: The Second Workshop on Evaluating Vector Space Representations for NLP*. Association for Computational Linguistics.

Jeffrey Pennington, Richard Socher, and Christopher Manning. 2014. Glove: Global vectors for word representation. In *Proceedings of the 2014 Conference on Empirical Methods in Natural Language Processing (EMNLP)*. Association for Computational Linguistics, pages 1532–1543. https://doi.org/10.3115/v1/D14-1162.

Ivan Vendrov, Ryan Kiros, Sanja Fidler, and Raquel Urtasun. 2015. Order-embeddings of images and language. *CoRR* abs/1511.06361. http://arxiv.org/abs/1511.06361.

Adina Williams, Nikita Nangia, and Samuel R. Bowman. 2017. A broad-coverage challenge corpus for sentence understanding through inference. *CoRR* abs/1704.05426. http://arxiv.org/abs/1704.05426.

Junbei Zhang, Xiaodan Zhu, Qian Chen, Lirong Dai, Si Wei, and Hui Jiang. 2017. Exploring question understanding and adaptation in neural-network-based question answering. *CoRR* abs/arXiv:1703.04617v2. https://arxiv.org/abs/1703.04617.

Shortcut-Stacked Sentence Encoders for Multi-Domain Inference

Yixin Nie and **Mohit Bansal**
UNC Chapel Hill
{yixin1, mbansal}@cs.unc.edu

Abstract

We present a simple sequential sentence encoder for multi-domain natural language inference. Our encoder is based on stacked bidirectional LSTM-RNNs with shortcut connections and fine-tuning of word embeddings. The overall supervised model uses the above encoder to encode two input sentences into two vectors, and then uses a classifier over the vector combination to label the relationship between these two sentences as that of entailment, contradiction, or neural. Our Shortcut-Stacked sentence encoders achieve strong improvements over existing encoders on matched and mismatched multi-domain natural language inference (top single-model result in the EMNLP RepEval 2017 Shared Task (Nangia et al., 2017)). Moreover, they achieve the new state-of-the-art encoding result on the original SNLI dataset (Bowman et al., 2015).

1 Introduction and Background

Natural language inference (NLI) or recognizing textual entailment (RTE) is a fundamental semantic task in the field of natural language processing. The problem is to determine whether a given hypothesis sentence can be logically inferred from a given premise sentence. Recently released datasets such as the Stanford Natural Language Inference Corpus (Bowman et al., 2015) (SNLI) and the Multi-Genre Natural Language Inference Corpus (Williams et al., 2017) (Multi-NLI) have not only encouraged several end-to-end neural network approaches to NLI, but have also served as an evaluation resource for general representation learning of natural language.

Depending on whether a model will first encode a sentence into a fixed-length vector without any incorporating information from the other sentence, the several proposed models can be categorized into two groups: (1) encoding-based models (or sentence encoders), such as Tree-based CNN encoders (TBCNN) in Mou et al. (2015) or Stack-augmented Parser-Interpreter Neural Network (SPINN) in Bowman et al. (2016), and (2) joint, pairwise models that use cross-features between the two sentences to encode them, such as the Enhanced Sequential Inference Model (ESIM) in Chen et al. (2017) or the bilateral multi-perspective matching (BiMPM) model Wang et al. (2017). Moreover, common sentence encoders can again be classified into tree-based encoders such as SPINN in Bowman et al. (2016) which we mentioned before, or sequential encoders such as the biLSTM model by Bowman et al. (2015).

In this paper, we follow the former approach of encoding-based models, and propose a novel yet simple sequential sentence encoder for the Multi-NLI problem. Our encoder does not require any syntactic information of the sentence. It also does not contain any attention or memory structure. It is basically a stacked (multi-layered) bidirectional LSTM-RNN with shortcut connections (feeding all previous layers' outputs and word embeddings to each layer) and word embedding fine-tuning. The overall supervised model uses these shortcut-stacked encoders to encode two input sentences into two vectors, and then we use a classifier over the vector combination to label the relationship between these two sentences as that of entailment, contradiction, or neural (similar to the classifier setup of Bowman et al. (2015) and Conneau et al. (2017)). Our simple shortcut-stacked encoders achieve strong improvements over existing encoders due to its multi-layered and shortcut-connected properties, on both matched and mis-

Proceedings of the 2nd Workshop on Evaluating Vector-Space Representations for NLP, pages 41–45,
Copenhagen, Denmark, September 7–11, 2017. ©2017 Association for Computational Linguistics

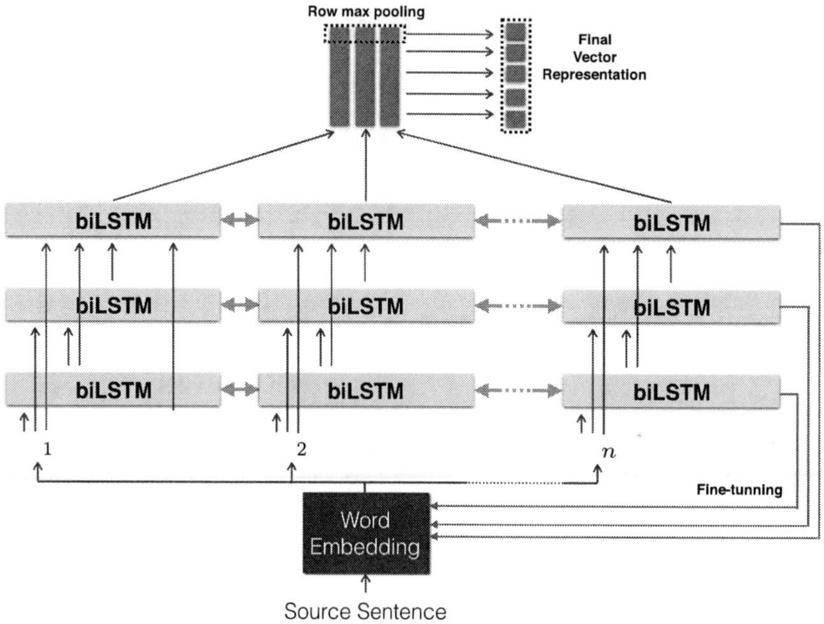

Figure 1: Our encoder's architecture: stacked biLSTM with shortcut connections and fine-tuning.

matched evaluation settings for multi-domain natural language inference, as well as on the original SNLI dataset. It is the top single-model (non-ensemble) result in the EMNLP RepEval 2017 Multi-NLI Shared Task (Nangia et al., 2017), and the new state-of-the-art for encoding-based results on the SNLI dataset (Bowman et al., 2015).

Github Code Link: `https://github.com/easonnie/multiNLI_encoder`

2 Model

Our model mainly consists of two separate components, a sentence encoder and an entailment classifier. The sentence encoder compresses each source sentence into a vector representation and the classifier makes a three-way classification based on the two vectors of the two source sentences. The model follows the 'encoding-based rule', i.e., the encoder will encode each source sentence into a fixed length vector without any information or function based on the other sentence (e.g., cross-attention or memory comparing the two sentences). In order to fully explore the generalization of the sentence encoder, the same encoder is applied to both the premise and the hypothesis with shared parameters projecting them into the same space. This setting follows the idea of Siamese Networks in Bromley et al. (1994). Figure 1 shows the overview of our encoding model (the standard classifier setup is not shown here; see Bowman et al. (2015) and Conneau et al. (2017) for that).

2.1 Sentence Encoder

Our sentence encoder is simply composed of multiple stacked bidirectional LSTM (biLSTM) layers with shortcut connections followed by a max pooling layer. Let bilstm^i represent the ith biLSTM layer, which is defined as:

$$h_t^i = \text{bilstm}^i(x_t^i, t), \forall t \in [1, 2, ..., n] \quad (1)$$

where h_t^i is the output of the ith biLSTM at time t over input sequence $(x_1^i, x_2^i, ..., x_n^i)$.

In a typical **stacked biLSTM** structure, the input of the next LSTM-RNN layer is simply the output sequence of the previous LSTM-RNN layer. In our settings, the input sequences for the ith biLSTM layer are the concatenated outputs of *all the previous layers*, plus the original word embedding sequence. This gives a **shortcut connection** style setup, related to the widely used idea of residual connections in CNNs for computer vision (He et al., 2016), highway networks for RNNs in speech processing (Zhang et al., 2016), and shortcut connections in hierarchical multitasking learning (Hashimoto et al., 2016); but in our case we feed in all the previous layers' output sequences as well as the word embedding sequence to every layer.

Let $W = (w_1, w_2, ..., w_n)$ represent words in the source sentence. We assume $w_i \in \mathbb{R}^d$ is a word embedding vector which are initialized using some pre-trained vector embeddings (and is then fine-tuned end-to-end via the NLI supervision). Then, the input of ith biLSTM layer at time t is defined as:

$$x_t^1 = w_t \tag{2}$$

$$x_t^i = [w_t, h_t^{i-1}, h_t^{i-2}, ...h_t^1] \quad (\text{for } i > 1) \tag{3}$$

where [] represents vector concatenation.

Then, assuming we have m layers of biLSTM, the final vector representation will be obtained by applying row-max-pool over the output of the last biLSTM layer, similar to Conneau et al. (2017). The final layer is defined as:

$$H^m = (h_1^m, h_2^m, ..., h_n^m) \tag{4}$$

$$v = max(H^m) \tag{5}$$

where $h_i^m, v \in \mathbb{R}^{2d_m}$, $H^m \in \mathbb{R}^{2d_m \times n}$, d_m is the dimension of the hidden state of the last forward and backward LSTM layers, and v is the final vector representation for the source sentence (which is later fed to the NLI classifier).

The closest encoder architecture to ours is that of Conneau et al. (2017), whose model consists of a single-layer biLSTM with a max-pooling layer, which we treat as our starting point. Our experiments (Section 4) demonstrate that our enhancements of the stacked-biRNN with shortcut connections provide significant gains on top of this baseline (for both SNLI and Multi-NLI).

2.2 Entailment Classifier

After we obtain the vector representation for the premise and hypothesis sentence, we apply three matching methods to the two vectors (i) concatenation (ii) element-wise distance and (iii) element-wise product for these two vectors and then concatenate these three match vectors (based on the heuristic matching presented in Mou et al. (2015)). Let v_p and v_h be the vector representations for premise and hypothesis, respectively. The matching vector is then defined as:

$$m = [v_p, v_h, |v_p - v_h|, v_p \otimes v_h] \tag{6}$$

At last, we feed this final concatenated result m into a MLP layer and use a softmax layer to make final classification.

Layers and Dimensions		Accuracy	
#layers	bilstm-dim	Matched	Mismatched
1	512	72.5	72.9
2	512 + 512	73.4	73.6
1	1024	72.9	72.9
2	512 + 1024	73.7	74.2
1	2048	73.0	73.5
2	512 + 2048	73.7	74.2
2	1024 + 2048	73.8	74.4
2	2048 + 2048	74.0	74.6
3	512 + 1024 + 2048	**74.2**	**74.7**

Table 1: Analysis of results for models with different # of biLSTM layers and their hidden state dimensions.

	Matched	Mismatched
without any shortcut connection	72.6	73.4
only word shortcut connection	74.2	74.6
full shortcut connection	**74.2**	**74.7**

Table 2: Ablation results with and without shortcut connections.

Word-Embedding	Matched	Mismatched
fixed	71.8	72.6
fine-tuned	**72.7**	**72.8**

Table 3: Ablation results with and without fine-tuning of word embeddings.

# of MLPs	Activation	Matched	Mismatched
1	tanh	73.7	74.1
2	tanh	73.5	73.6
1	relu	74.1	74.7
2	relu	**74.2**	**74.7**

Table 4: Ablation results for different MLP classifiers.

3 Experimental Setup

3.1 Datasets

As instructed in the RepEval Multi-NLI shared task, we use all of the training data in Multi-NLI combined with 15% randomly selected samples from the SNLI training set resampled at each epoch) as our final training set for all models; and we use both the cross-domain ('mismatched') and in-domain ('matched') Multi-NLI development sets for model selection. For the SNLI test results in Table 5, we train on only the SNLI training set (and we also verify that the tuning decisions hold true on the SNLI dev set).

3.2 Parameter Settings

We use cross-entropy loss as the training objective with Adam-based (Kingma and Ba, 2014) opti-

Model	Accuracy		
	SNLI	Multi-NLI Matched	Multi-NLI Mismatched
CBOW (Williams et al., 2017)	80.6	65.2	64.6
biLSTM Encoder (Williams et al., 2017)	81.5	67.5	67.1
300D Tree-CNN Encoder (Mou et al., 2015)	82.1	–	–
300D SPINN-PI Encoder (Bowman et al., 2016)	83.2	–	–
300D NSE Encoder (Munkhdalai and Yu, 2016)	84.6	–	–
biLSTM-Max Encoder (Conneau et al., 2017)	84.5	–	–
Our biLSTM-Max Encoder	85.2	71.7	71.2
Our Shortcut-Stacked Encoder	**86.1**	**74.6**	**73.6**

Table 5: Final Test Results on SNLI and Multi-NLI datasets.

mization with 32 batch size. The starting learning rate is 0.0002 with half decay every two epochs. The number of hidden units for MLP in classifier is 1600. Dropout layer is also applied on the output of each layer of MLP, with dropout rate set to 0.1. We used pre-trained 300D Glove 840B vectors (Pennington et al., 2014) to initialize the word embeddings. Tuning decisions for word embedding training strategy, the hyperparameters of dimension and number of layers for biLSTM, and the activation type and number of layers for MLP, are all explained in Section 4.

4 Results and Analysis

4.1 Ablation Analysis Results

We now investigate the effectiveness of each of the enhancement components in our overall model. These ablation results are shown in Tables 1, 2, 3 and 4, all based on the Multi-NLI development sets. Finally, Table 5 shows results for different encoders on SNLI and Multi-NLI test sets.

First, Table 1 shows the performance changes for different number of biLSTM layers and their varying dimension size. The dimension size of a biLSTM layer is referring to the dimension of the hidden state for both the forward and backward LSTM-RNNs. As shown, each added layer model improves the accuracy and we achieve a substantial improvement in accuracy (around 2%) on both matched and mismatched settings, compared to the single-layer biLSTM in Conneau et al. (2017). We only experimented with up to 3 layers with 512, 1024, 2048 dimensions each, so the model still has potential to improve the result further with a larger dimension and more layers.

Next, in Table 2, we show that the shortcut connections among the biLSTM layers is also an important contributor to accuracy improvement (around 1.5% on top of the full 3-layered stacked-RNN model). This demonstrates that simply stacking the biLSTM layers is not sufficient to handle a complex task like Multi-NLI and it is significantly better to have the higher layer connected to both the output and the original input of all the previous layers (note that Table 1 results are based on multi-layered models with shortcut connections).

Next, in Table 3, we show that fine-tuning the word embeddings also improves results, again for both the in-domain task and cross-domain tasks (the ablation results are based on a smaller model with a 128+256 2-layer biLSTM). Hence, all our models were trained with word embeddings being fine-tuned. The last ablation in Table 4 shows that a classifier with two layers of relu is preferable than other options. Thus, we use that setting for our strongest encoder.

4.2 Multi-NLI and SNLI Test Results

Finally, in Table 5, we report the test results for MNLI and SNLI. First for Multi-NLI, we improve substantially over the CBOW and biLSTM Encoder baselines reported in the dataset paper (Williams et al., 2017). We also show that our final shortcut-based stacked encoder achieves around 3% improvement as compared to the 1-layer biLSTM-Max Encoder in the second last row (using the exact same classifier and optimizer settings). Our shortcut-encoder was also the top singe-model (non-ensemble) result on the EMNLP RepEval Shared Task leaderboard.

Next, for SNLI, we compare our shortcut-stacked encoder with the current state-of-the-art encoders from the SNLI leaderboard (`https://nlp.stanford.edu/projects/snli/`). We also compare to the recent biLSTM-Max Encoder of Conneau et al. (2017), which served as our model's 1-layer starting point.[1] The results indicate that 'Our Shortcut-Stacked Encoder' sur-

[1]Note that the 'Our biLSTM-Max Encoder' results in the second-last row are obtained using our reimplementation of the Conneau et al. (2017) model; our version is 0.7% better, likely due to our classifier and optimizer settings.

passes all the previous state-of-the-art encoders, and achieves the new best encoding-based result on SNLI, suggesting the general effectiveness of simple shortcut-connected stacked layers in sentence encoders.

5 Conclusion

We explored various simple combinations and connections of biLSTM-RNN layered architectures and developed a Shortcut-Stacked Sentence Encoder for natural language inference. Our model is the top single result in the EMNLP RepEval 2017 Multi-NLI Shared Task, and it also surpasses the state-of-the-art encoders for the SNLI dataset. In future work, we are also evaluating the effectiveness of shortcut-stacked sentence encoders on several other semantic tasks.

Acknowledgments

We thank the shared task organizers and the anonymous reviewers. This work was partially supported by a Google Faculty Research Award, an IBM Faculty Award, a Bloomberg Data Science Research Grant, and NVidia GPU awards.

References

Samuel R. Bowman, Gabor Angeli, Christopher Potts, and Christopher D. Manning. 2015. A large annotated corpus for learning natural language inference. In *Proceedings of the 2015 Conference on Empirical Methods in Natural Language Processing (EMNLP)*. Association for Computational Linguistics.

Samuel R Bowman, Jon Gauthier, Abhinav Rastogi, Raghav Gupta, Christopher D Manning, and Christopher Potts. 2016. A fast unified model for parsing and sentence understanding. *arXiv preprint arXiv:1603.06021* .

Jane Bromley, Isabelle Guyon, Yann LeCun, Eduard Säckinger, and Roopak Shah. 1994. Signature verification using a "Siamese" time delay neural network. In *Advances in Neural Information Processing Systems*. pages 737–744.

Qian Chen, Xiaodan Zhu, Zhen-Hua Ling, Si Wei, Hui Jiang, and Diana Inkpen. 2017. Enhanced lstm for natural language inference. In *Proc. ACL*.

Alexis Conneau, Douwe Kiela, Holger Schwenk, Loic Barrault, and Antoine Bordes. 2017. Supervised learning of universal sentence representations from natural language inference data. *arXiv preprint arXiv:1705.02364* .

Kazuma Hashimoto, Caiming Xiong, Yoshimasa Tsuruoka, and Richard Socher. 2016. A joint many-task model: Growing a neural network for multiple nlp tasks. *arXiv preprint arXiv:1611.01587* .

Kaiming He, Xiangyu Zhang, Shaoqing Ren, and Jian Sun. 2016. Deep residual learning for image recognition. In *Proceedings of the IEEE Conference on Computer Vision and Pattern Recognition*. pages 770–778.

Diederik Kingma and Jimmy Ba. 2014. Adam: A method for stochastic optimization. *arXiv preprint arXiv:1412.6980* .

Lili Mou, Rui Men, Ge Li, Yan Xu, Lu Zhang, Rui Yan, and Zhi Jin. 2015. Natural language inference by tree-based convolution and heuristic matching. *arXiv preprint arXiv:1512.08422* .

Tsendsuren Munkhdalai and Hong Yu. 2016. Neural semantic encoders. *arXiv preprint arXiv:1607.04315* .

Nikita Nangia, Adina Williams, Angeliki Lazaridou, and Samuel R. Bowman. 2017. The repeval 2017 shared task: Multi-genre natural language inference with sentence representations. In *Proceedings of RepEval 2017: The Second Workshop on Evaluating Vector Space Representations for NLP*. Association for Computational Linguistics.

Jeffrey Pennington, Richard Socher, and Christopher D. Manning. 2014. Glove: Global vectors for word representation. In *Empirical Methods in Natural Language Processing (EMNLP)*. pages 1532–1543. http://www.aclweb.org/anthology/D14-1162.

Zhiguo Wang, Wael Hamza, and Radu Florian. 2017. Bilateral multi-perspective matching for natural language sentences. *arXiv preprint arXiv:1702.03814* .

Adina Williams, Nikita Nangia, and Samuel R Bowman. 2017. A broad-coverage challenge corpus for sentence understanding through inference. *arXiv preprint arXiv:1704.05426* .

Yu Zhang, Guoguo Chen, Dong Yu, Kaisheng Yaco, Sanjeev Khudanpur, and James Glass. 2016. Highway long short-term memory rnns for distant speech recognition. In *Acoustics, Speech and Signal Processing (ICASSP), 2016 IEEE International Conference on*. IEEE, pages 5755–5759.

Character-level Intra Attention Network for Natural Language Inference

Han Yang and **Marta R. Costa-jussà** and **José A. R. Fonollosa**
TALP Research Center
Universitat Politècnica de Catalunya
han.yang@est.fib.upc.edu {marta.ruiz, jose.fonollosa}@upc.edu

Abstract

Natural language inference (NLI) is a central problem in language understanding. End-to-end artificial neural networks have reached state-of-the-art performance in NLI field recently.

In this paper, we propose Character-level Intra Attention Network (CIAN) for the NLI task. In our model, we use the character-level convolutional network to replace the standard word embedding layer, and we use the intra attention to capture the intra-sentence semantics. The proposed CIAN model provides improved results based on a newly published MNLI corpus.

1 Introduction

Natural language inference in natural language processing refers to the problem of determining a directional relation between two text fragments. Given a sentence pair (premise, hypothesis), the task is to predict whether hypothesis is entailed by premise, hypothesis is contradicted to premise, or whether the relation between premise and hypothesis is neutral.

Recently, the dominating trend of works in natural language processing is based on artificial neural networks, which aims at building deep and complex encoder to transform a sentence into encoded vectors. For instance, there are recurrent neural network (RNN) based encoders, which recursively concatenate each word with its previous memory, until the whole information of a sentence has been derived. The most common RNN encoders are Long Short-Term Memory Networks (LSTM; Hochreiter and Schmidhuber, 1997) and Gated Recurrent Unit (Chung et al., 2014). RNNs have surpassed the performance of traditional baselines in many NLP tasks (Dai and Le, 2015). There are also convolutional neural network (CNN; LeCun et al., 1989) based encoders, which concatenate the sentence information by applying multiple convolving filters over the sentence. CNNs have achieved state-of-the-art results on various NLP tasks (Collobert et al., 2011).

To evaluate the quality of the NLI model, the Stanford Natural Language Inference (SNLI; Bowman et al., 2015) corpus of 570K sentence pairs was introduced. It serves as a standard benchmark for NLI task. However, most of the sentences in SNLI corpus are short and simple, which limit the room for fine-grained comparisons between models. Currently, a more comprehensive Multi-Genre NLI corpus (MNLI; Williams et al., 2017) of 433K sentence pairs was released, aiming at evaluating large-scale NLI models. Authors gave out some baseline results accompanied by the publish of MNLI corpus, the BiLSTM model achieves an accuracy of 67.5, and the Enhanced Sequential Inference Model (Chen et al., 2016) achieves an accuracy of 72.4.

Among those encoders for NLI task, most of them use word-level embedding, and initialize the weight of the embedding layer with pre-trained word vectors such as GloVe (Pennington et al., 2014). The pre-trained word vectors helps the encoders to catch richer semantic information. However, it also has its downside. As the growth of vocabulary size in the modern corpus, there will be more and more out-of-vocabulary (OOV) words that are not presented in the pre-trained word embedding vector. As the word-level embedding is blind to subword information (e.g. morphemes), it leads to high perplexities for those OOV words.

In this paper, we use the BiLSTM model from (Williams et al., 2017) as the baseline model for the evaluation of the MNLI corpus. To augment the baseline model, firstly, a character-level

Proceedings of the 2nd Workshop on Evaluating Vector-Space Representations for NLP, pages 46–50,
Copenhagen, Denmark, September 7–11, 2017. ©2017 Association for Computational Linguistics

convolutional neural network (CharCNN; Kim et al., 2016) is applied. We use the CharCNN to replace the word embedding layer in the baseline model, which will be computed from the characters of corresponding word. Secondly, the intra attention mechanism introduced by (Yang et al., 2016) will be applied, to enhance the model with a richer information of substructures of a sentence.

2 Model Development

2.1 BiLSTM Baseline

The baseline model we used here is introduced by (Williams et al., 2017) accompanied with the publication of MNLI corpus. It has a 5-layer structure which is shown in Figure 1.

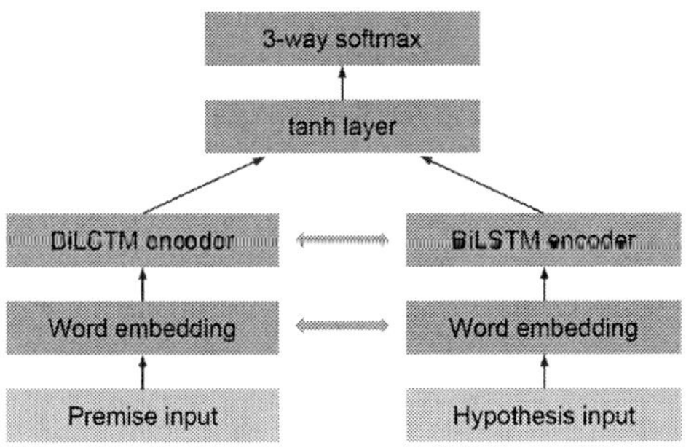

Figure 1: BiLSTM model architecture

In the baseline model, a word embedding layer initialized with pre-trained GloVe vectors (840B token version) is implemented to transform the input text into sequence of word vectors. OOV words are initialized randomly. Then, the sentence representation vector h is produced by implementing an average pooling over the BiLSTM hidden states $[h_0, h_1, \cdots, h_n]$. Finally, the concatenation of encoded premise and hypothesis representation vector is passed through a tanh layer followed by a three-way softmax classifier to attain the label prediction.

2.2 Character-level Convolutional Neural Network

In the baseline model, the input x_t to the BiLSTM encoder layer at time t is sequence of pre-trained word embeddings. Those pre-trained word embeddings can boost the performance of the model. However, it is limited to the finite-size of vocabulary. Here we replace the word embedding layer with a character-level convolutional neural network (CharCNN; Kim et al., 2016) for language modeling, which also achieved success in machine translation (Costa-Jussà and Fonollosa, 2016).

We define the text sentence input as vector $C^k \in R^{d \times l}$, where $k \in K$ is the k-th word in a sentence, d is the dimensionality of character embeddings, l is the length of characters in k-th word. Then a set of narrow convolutions between C^k and filter H is applied, followed with a max-over-time (max pooling) as shown in Equation 1-2.

$$f^k[i] = \tanh(\langle C^k[*, i : i + \omega - 1], H\rangle + b) \quad (1)$$

$$y^k = \max_i f^k[i] \quad (2)$$

The concatenation of those max pooling values y^k provides us with a representation vector y of each sentence. Then, a highway network is applied upon y, as shown in Equation 3, where g is a nonlinear transformation, $t = \sigma(W_T y + b_T)$ is called the transform gate, and $(1 - t)$ is called the carry gate. Highway layers allow for training of deep networks by adaptively carrying some dimensions of the input y directly to the output z.

$$z = t \odot g(W_H y + b_H) + (1 - t) \odot y \quad (3)$$

Experiment conducted by (Kim et al., 2016) has shown that the CNN layer can extract the orthographic features of words (e.g. *German* and *Germany*). It has also been shown that highway layer is able to encode semantic features that are not discernable from orthography alone. For instance, after highway layers the nearest neighbor word of *you* is *we*, which is orthographically distinct from *you*.

2.3 Intra Attention Mechanism

In the baseline model, the BiLSTM encoder takes an average pooling over all its hidden states to produce a single representation vector of each sentence. However, this has its bottleneck as we intuitively know that not all words (hidden states) contribute equally to the sentence representation. To augment the performance of RNN based encoder, the concept of attention mechanism was introduced by (Bahdanau et al., 2014) for machine translation. Attention mechanism is a hidden layer which computes a categorical distribution to make a soft-selection over source elements (Kim et al., 2017). It has recently demonstrated success on tasks such as parsing text (Vinyals et al., 2015), sentence summarization (Rush et al., 2015) and also on a wide range of NLP tasks (Cheng et al., 2016).

Here we implemented the Intra Attention mechanism introduced by (Yang et al., 2016) for document classification. We define the hidden states as the output of the BiLSTM encoder as $h_t \in [h_0, h_1, \cdots, h_n]$, the intra attention is applied upon the hidden states to get the sentence representation vector h, specifically,

$$u_t = \tanh(W_\omega h_t + b_\omega) \tag{4}$$

$$\alpha_t = \frac{exp(u_t^T u_\omega)}{\sum_t exp(u_t^T u_\omega)} \tag{5}$$

$$h = \sum_t \alpha_t h_t \tag{6}$$

It first feed all hidden states h_t through a nonlinearity to get u_t as the hidden representation of h_t. Then it uses a $softmax$ function to catch the normalized importance weight matrix α_t. After that, the sentence representation vector h is computed by a weighted sum of all hidden states h_t with the weight matrix α_t. The context vector u_ω can be seen as a high-level representation of the importance of informative words.

2.4 Character-level Intra Attention Network

The overall architecture of the Character-level Intra Attention Network (CIAN) is shown in Figure 2. The CIAN model is consisted with 7 layers, of which the first and the last layers are the same with our baseline model. The 4 layers in middle are our augmented layers that has been introduced in this section.

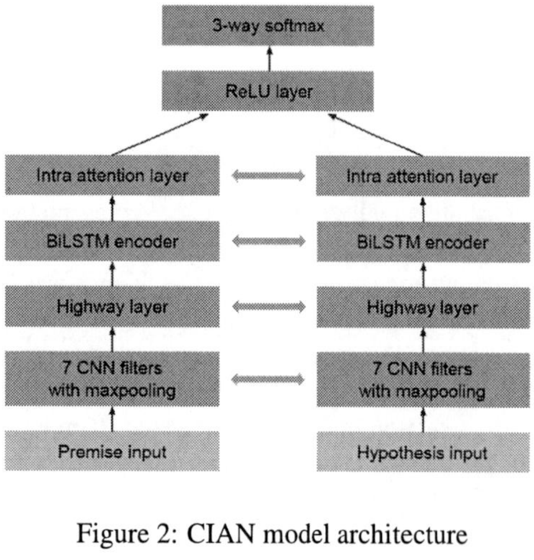

Figure 2: CIAN model architecture

The input text is firstly set to lowercase, then it is vectorized according to the tokenization list [abcdefghijklmnopqrstuvwxyz0123456789,;.!?:'"()[]{}]. Those characters not in the list are initialized with a vector of zero. After that we use 7 filters in CIAN model's CNN layer. The widths of the CNN filters are $w = [1, 2, 3, 4, 5, 6, 7]$, and the corresponding filters' size are $[\min\{200, 50 \cdot w\}]$. Two highway layers are implemented following the CNN layer. The attention layer uses weighted sum of all hidden states h_t with the attention weight matrix α_t to encode each sentence into a fixed-length sentence representation vector. Finally a ReLU layer and a three-way softmax classifier use those representation vectors to conduct the prediction.

3 Experiments

3.1 Data

We evaluated our approach on the Multi-Genre NLI (MNLI) corpus, as a shared task for RepEval 2017 workshop (Nangia et al., 2017). We train our CIAN model on a mixture of MNLI and SNLI corpus, by using a full MNLI training set and a randomly selected 20 percent of the SNLI training set at each epoch.

3.2 Hyper Parameters

The BiLSTM encoder layer use 300D hidden states, thus 600D as its a bidirectional encoder. Dropout (Srivastava et al., 2014) is implemented with a dropout rate of 0.2 to prevent the model from overfitting. Parameter weights for premise encoder and hypothesis encoder are shared using siamese architecture. The Adam optimizer (Kingma and Ba, 2014) is used for training with backpropagation.

The model has been implemented using Keras and we have released the code [1]. The training took approximately one hour for one epoch on GeForce GTX TITAN, and we stopped training after 40 epochs as an early stopping regularization.

3.3 Result

We compared the results of CIAN model with the results of BiLSTM model given by (Williams et al., 2017). Table 1 shows that the accuracy is improved by 0.9 percent in matched test set, and 0.6 percent in mismatched test set.

[1]https://github.com/yanghanxy/CIAN

Model	Matched	Mismatched
BiLSTM	67.0	67.6
CIAN	67.9	68.2

Table 1: Test set accuracies (%) on MNLI corpus.

	Matched		Mismatched	
Tag	BiLSTM	CIAN	BiLSTM	CIAN
CONDITIONAL	100	48	100	62
WORD_OVERLAP	50	79	57	62
NEGATION	71	71	69	70
ANTO	67	82	58	70
LONG_SENTENCE	50	68	55	63
TENCE_DIFFERNCE	64	65	71	72
ACTIVE/PASSIVE	75	87	82	90
PARAPHRASE	78	88	81	89
QUANTITY/TIME	50	47	46	44
COREF	84	67	80	72
QUANTIFIER	64	63	70	69
MODAL	66	66	64	70
BELIEF	74	71	73	70

Table 2: Accuracies (%) on matched and mismatched expert-tagged development data.

We conducted error analysis based on expert-tagged development data released by the organizers of RepEval 2017 shared task. The results are shown in Table 2. From the results, it can be seen that the accuracy for WORD_OVERLAP, LONG_SENTENCE, ACTIVE/PASSIVE and PARAPHRASE have been improved significantly in both matched and mismatched development set. While the accuracy for CONDITIONAL and COREF haven been decreased in both development set.

We also conducted visualization on the attention weights α_t of the intra attention layer. By doing so, we we can understand how the model judges the NLI relation between two sentences.

Figure 3 is visualizations of attention weights for 2 sentence pairs, with premise at left and hypothesis at right. Each word is attained with a color block. The darker the color, the greater the attention weight, which means the higher importance contributed to the sentence representation.

From the Visualization, it could be seen that the model has more attention on words with similar semantic meaning (e.g. *love* and *enjoy*), and the model applies more attention on overlapped words (e.g. *efficiencies* and *efficiencies*).

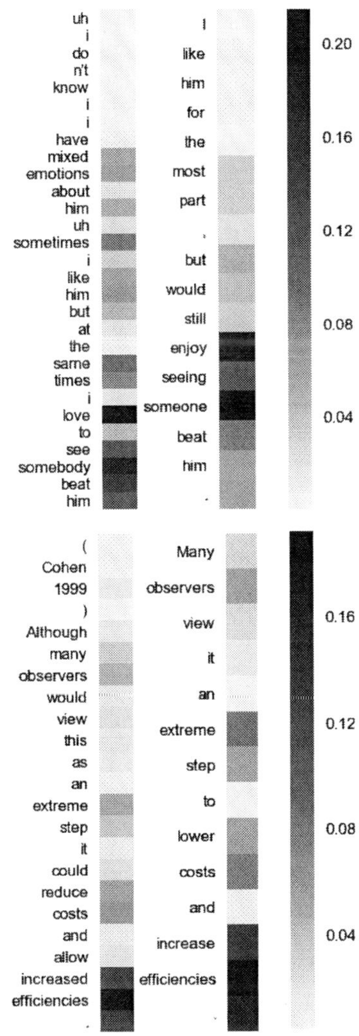

Figure 3: Visualization of attention weights of sentence pair 254941e (top) and 192997e (bottom)

4 Conclusion

In this paper, we presented a Character-level Intra Attention Network (CIAN) for the task of natural language inference. Experimental results demonstrate that our model slightly outperforms the baseline model upon the MultiNLI corpus. The CharCNN layers helps the model to capture rich semantic and orthographic features. The intra attention layer augment the model's ability to efficiently encode long sentences, and it enhances the models' interpretability by visualizing the attention weights.

In general, the model presented in this paper is a sequence encoder that do not need any specific pre-processing or outside data like pre-trained word embeddings. Thus, it can be easily applied to other autoencoder architecture tasks such as language modeling, sentiment analysis and question answering.

Acknowledgments

This work is supported by the Spanish Ministerio de Economía y Competitividad and Fondo Europeo de Desarrollo Regional through contract TEC2015-69266-P (MINECO/FEDER, UE), by the postdoctoral senior grant Ramón y Cajal, and by the China Scholarship Council (CSC) under grant No.201506890038.

References

Dzmitry Bahdanau, Kyunghyun Cho, and Yoshua Bengio. 2014. Neural machine translation by jointly learning to align and translate. *CoRR* abs/1409.0473.

Samuel R. Bowman, Gabor Angeli, Christopher Potts, and Christopher D. Manning. 2015. A large annotated corpus for learning natural language inference. In *Proceedings of the 2015 Conference on Empirical Methods in Natural Language Processing, EMNLP 2015*. pages 632–642.

Qian Chen, Xiaodan Zhu, Zhen-Hua Ling, Si Wei, and Hui Jiang. 2016. Enhancing and combining sequential and tree LSTM for natural language inference. *CoRR* abs/1609.06038.

Jianpeng Cheng, Li Dong, and Mirella Lapata. 2016. Long short-term memory-networks for machine reading. In *Proceedings of the 2016 Conference on Empirical Methods in Natural Language Processing, EMNLP 2016*. pages 551–561.

Junyoung Chung, Çaglar Gülçehre, KyungHyun Cho, and Yoshua Bengio. 2014. Empirical evaluation of gated recurrent neural networks on sequence modeling. *CoRR* abs/1412.3555.

Ronan Collobert, Jason Weston, Léon Bottou, Michael Karlen, Koray Kavukcuoglu, and Pavel P. Kuksa. 2011. Natural language processing (almost) from scratch. *Journal of Machine Learning Research* 12:2493–2537.

Marta R. Costa-Jussà and José A. R. Fonollosa. 2016. Character-based neural machine translation. In *Proceedings of the 54th Annual Meeting of the Association for Computational Linguistics, ACL 2016, Volume 2: Short Papers*.

Andrew M. Dai and Quoc V. Le. 2015. Semi-supervised sequence learning. In *Advances in Neural Information Processing Systems 28: Annual Conference on Neural Information Processing Systems 2015*. pages 3079–3087.

Sepp Hochreiter and Jürgen Schmidhuber. 1997. Long short-term memory. *Neural Computation* 9(8):1735–1780.

Yoon Kim, Carl Denton, Luong Hoang, and Alexander M. Rush. 2017. Structured attention networks. *CoRR* abs/1702.00887.

Yoon Kim, Yacine Jernite, David Sontag, and Alexander M. Rush. 2016. Character-aware neural language models. In *Proceedings of the Thirtieth AAAI Conference on Artificial Intelligence*. pages 2741–2749.

Diederik P. Kingma and Jimmy Ba. 2014. Adam: A method for stochastic optimization. *CoRR* abs/1412.6980.

Yann LeCun, John S. Denker, and Sara A. Solla. 1989. Optimal brain damage. In *Advances in Neural Information Processing Systems 2, [NIPS Conference, 1989]*. pages 598–605.

Nikita Nangia, Adina Williams, Angeliki Lazaridou, and Samuel R. Bowman. 2017. The repeval 2017 shared task: Multi-genre natural language inference with sentence representations. In *Proceedings of RepEval 2017: The Second Workshop on Evaluating Vector Space Representations for NLP*. Association for Computational Linguistics.

Jeffrey Pennington, Richard Socher, and Christopher D. Manning. 2014. Glove: Global vectors for word representation. In *Proceedings of the 2014 Conference on Empirical Methods in Natural Language Processing, EMNLP 2014, A meeting of SIGDAT, a Special Interest Group of the ACL*. pages 1532–1543.

Alexander M. Rush, Sumit Chopra, and Jason Weston. 2015. A neural attention model for abstractive sentence summarization. In *Proceedings of the 2015 Conference on Empirical Methods in Natural Language Processing, EMNLP 2015*. pages 379–389.

Nitish Srivastava, Geoffrey E. Hinton, Alex Krizhevsky, Ilya Sutskever, and Ruslan Salakhutdinov. 2014. Dropout: a simple way to prevent neural networks from overfitting. *Journal of Machine Learning Research* 15(1):1929–1958.

Oriol Vinyals, Lukasz Kaiser, Terry Koo, Slav Petrov, Ilya Sutskever, and Geoffrey E. Hinton. 2015. Grammar as a foreign language. In *Advances in Neural Information Processing Systems 28: Annual Conference on Neural Information Processing Systems 2015*. pages 2773–2781.

Adina Williams, Nikita Nangia, and Samuel R. Bowman. 2017. A broad-coverage challenge corpus for sentence understanding through inference. *CoRR* abs/1704.05426.

Zichao Yang, Diyi Yang, Chris Dyer, Xiaodong He, Alexander J. Smola, and Eduard H. Hovy. 2016. Hierarchical attention networks for document classification. In *NAACL HLT 2016, The 2016 Conference of the North American Chapter of the Association for Computational Linguistics: Human Language Technologies*. pages 1480–1489.

Refining Raw Sentence Representations for Textual Entailment Recognition via Attention

Jorge A. Balazs, Edison Marrese-Taylor, Pablo Loyola, Yutaka Matsuo
Graduate School of Engineering
The University of Tokyo
{jorge,emarrese,pablo,matsuo}@weblab.t.u-tokyo.ac.jp

Abstract

In this paper we present the model used by the team Rivercorners for the 2017 RepEval shared task. First, our model separately encodes a pair of sentences into variable-length representations by using a bidirectional LSTM. Later, it creates fixed-length raw representations by means of simple aggregation functions, which are then refined using an attention mechanism. Finally it combines the refined representations of both sentences into a single vector to be used for classification. With this model we obtained test accuracies of 72.057% and 72.055% in the matched and mismatched evaluation tracks respectively, outperforming the LSTM baseline, and obtaining performances similar to a model that relies on shared information between sentences (ESIM). When using an ensemble both accuracies increased to 72.247% and 72.827% respectively.

1 Introduction

The task of Natural Language Inference (NLI) aims at characterizing the semantic concepts of entailment and contradiction, and is essential in tasks ranging from information retrieval to semantic parsing to commonsense reasoning, as both entailment and contradiction are central concepts in natural language meaning (Katz, 1972; van Benthem, 2008).

The aforementioned task has been addressed with a variety of techniques, including those based on symbolic logic, knowledge bases, and neural networks. With the advent of deep learning techniques, NLI has become an important testing ground for approaches that employ distributed word and phrase representations, which are typical of these models.

In this context, the Second Workshop on Evaluating Vector Space Representations for NLP (RepEval 2017) features a shared task meant to evaluate natural language understanding models based on sentence encoders by the means of NLI in the style of a three-class balanced classification problem over sentence pairs. The shared task includes two evaluations, a standard in-domain (matched) evaluation in which the training and test data are drawn from the same sources, and a cross-domain (mismatched) evaluation in which the training and test data differ substantially. This cross-domain evaluation is aimed at testing the ability of submitted systems to learn representations of sentence meaning that capture broadly useful features.

2 Proposed Model

Our work is related to intra-sentence attention models for sentence representation such as the ones described by Liu et al. (2016) and Lin et al. (2017). In particular, our model is based on the notion that, when reading a sentence, we usually need to re-read certain portions of it in order to obtain a comprehensive understanding. To model such phenomenon, we rely on an attention mechanism able to iteratively obtain a richer and more expressive version of a raw sentence representation. The model's architecture is described below:

Word Representation Layer: This layer is in charge of generating a comprehensive vector representation of each token for a given sentence. We construct this representation based on up to two basic components:

- Pre-trained word embeddings: We take pre-trained word embeddings and use them to generate a raw word representation. This can

Proceedings of the 2nd Workshop on Evaluating Vector-Space Representations for NLP, pages 51–55,
Copenhagen, Denmark, September 7–11, 2017. ©2017 Association for Computational Linguistics

be seen as a simple lookup-layer that returns a word vector for each provided word index.

- Character embeddings: We generate a character-based representation of each word, which we concatenate to the word vectors as returned by the previous component. We start by generating a randomly initialized character embedding matrix C. Then, we split each word into its component characters, get their corresponding character embedding vectors from C and feed them into a unidirectional Long Short-Term Memory Network (LSTM) (Hochreiter and Schmidhuber, 1997). We then choose the last hidden state returned by the LSTM as the fixed-size character-based vector representation for each token. Our embedding matrix C is trained with the rest of the model (Wang et al., 2017).

Context Representation Layer: This layer complements the vectors generated by the Word Representation Layer by incorporating contextual information into them. To do this, we utilize a bidirectional LSTM that reads through the embedded sequence and returns the hidden states for each time step. These are context-aware representations focused on each position. Formally, let S be a sentence such as $S = \{\boldsymbol{x}_1, \ldots, \boldsymbol{x}_n\}$, where each $\boldsymbol{x}_i$ is an embedded word vector as returned by the previous layer, then the context-rich word representation $\boldsymbol{h}_i$ is calculated as follows for each time step $i = 1, \ldots, n$:

$$\overrightarrow{\boldsymbol{h}}_i = LSTM(\boldsymbol{x}_i, \overrightarrow{\boldsymbol{h}}_{i-1}) \tag{1}$$

$$\overleftarrow{\boldsymbol{h}}_i = LSTM(\boldsymbol{x}_i, \overleftarrow{\boldsymbol{h}}_{i+1}) \tag{2}$$

$$\boldsymbol{h}_i = [\overrightarrow{\boldsymbol{h}}_i; \overleftarrow{\boldsymbol{h}}_i] \tag{3}$$

Where $\overrightarrow{\boldsymbol{h}}_i$ is the forward contextual vector representation of $\boldsymbol{x}_i$, $\overleftarrow{\boldsymbol{h}}_i$ the backward one, and $[\ \cdot\ ;\ \cdot\ ]$ represents the concatenation of two vectors. The output of this layer is a variable-length sentence representation for both the premise and hypothesis. We then define a pooling layer in charge of a generating a raw fixed-size representation of each sentence.

Pooling Layer: This layer is in charge of generating a crude sentence representation vector by reducing the sequence dimension using one of four simple operations, all of which are fed the context-aware token representations obtained previously:

$$\bar{\boldsymbol{h}} = \frac{1}{n}\sum_{i=1}^{n} \boldsymbol{h}_i \tag{4}$$

$$\bar{\boldsymbol{h}} = \sum_{i=1}^{n} \boldsymbol{h}_i \tag{5}$$

$$\bar{\boldsymbol{h}} = [\overrightarrow{\boldsymbol{h}}_n; \overleftarrow{\boldsymbol{h}}_1] \tag{6}$$

$$\bar{\boldsymbol{h}} = \max_{i=1\ldots n} \boldsymbol{h}_i \tag{7}$$

These operations correspond to the *mean* of the word representations (eq. 4), their *sum* (eq. 5), the concatenation of the *last* hidden state for each direction (eq. 6), and the *maximum* one (eq. 7).

Inner Attention Layer: To refine the representations generated by the pooling strategy, we use a global attention mechanism (Luong et al., 2015; Vinyals et al., 2015) that compares each context-aware token representation $\boldsymbol{h}_i$ with the raw sentence representation $\bar{\boldsymbol{h}}$. Formally,

$$u_i = \boldsymbol{v}^\top \tanh(W[\bar{\boldsymbol{h}}; \boldsymbol{h}_i]) \tag{8}$$

$$\alpha_i = \frac{\exp u_i}{\sum_{k=1}^{n} \exp u_k} \tag{9}$$

$$\bar{\boldsymbol{h}}' = \sum_{i=1}^{n} \alpha_i \boldsymbol{h}_i \tag{10}$$

Where both $\boldsymbol{v}$ and W are trainable parameters and $\bar{\boldsymbol{h}}'$ is the refined sentence representation[1].

Aggregation Layer: We apply two matching mechanisms to aggregate the refined sentence representations, which are directly aimed at extracting relationships between the premise and the hypothesis. Concretely, we concatenate the representations of the premise $\bar{\boldsymbol{h}}'_P$ and hypothesis $\bar{\boldsymbol{h}}'_H$ in addition to their element-wise product ($\odot$) and the absolute value ($|\cdot|$) of their difference, obtaining the vector $\boldsymbol{r}$. These last two operations, first proposed by Mou et al. (2015), can be seen as a sentence matching strategy.

$$\boldsymbol{h}_{mul} = \bar{\boldsymbol{h}}'_P \odot \bar{\boldsymbol{h}}'_H \tag{11}$$

$$\boldsymbol{h}_{dif} = |\bar{\boldsymbol{h}}'_P - \bar{\boldsymbol{h}}'_H| \tag{12}$$

$$\boldsymbol{r} = [\bar{\boldsymbol{h}}'_P; \bar{\boldsymbol{h}}'_H; \boldsymbol{h}_{mul}; \boldsymbol{h}_{dif}] \tag{13}$$

Dense Layer: Finally, $\boldsymbol{r}$ is fed to a fully-connected layer whose output is a vector containing the logits for each class, which are then fed to

[1]The refined sentence representation $\bar{\boldsymbol{h}}'$ for both premise and hypothesis is the final representation in which both are treated as separate entities. The representations produced by our best-performing model are available in `https://zenodo.org/record/825946`.

a softmax function for obtaining their probability distribution. The class with the highest probability is chosen as the predicted relationship between premise and hypothesis.

3 Experiments

To make our results comparable to the baselines reported in the Kaggle platform we randomly sampled 15% of the SNLI corpus (Bowman et al., 2015) and added it to the MultiNLI corpus.

We used the pre-trained 300-dimensional GloVe vectors trained on 840B tokens (Pennington et al., 2014). These embeddings were not fine-tuned during training and unknown word vectors were initialized by randomly sampling from the uniform distribution in $(-0.05, 0.05)$.

Each character embedding was initialized as a 20-dimensional vector and the character-level LSTM output dimension was set to 50. The word-level LSTM output dimension was set to 300, which means that after concatenating word-level and character-level representations the word vectors for each direction are 350-dimensional (i.e., $\boldsymbol{h}_i \in \mathbb{R}^{700}$).

For the Inner Attention Layer we defined the parameter W as a square matrix matching the dimension of the concatenated vector $[\bar{\boldsymbol{h}}; \boldsymbol{h}_i]$ (i.e., $W \in \mathbb{R}^{1400\times1400}$), and $\boldsymbol{v}$ as a vector matching the same dimension (i.e., $\boldsymbol{v} \in \mathbb{R}^{1400}$). Both W and $\boldsymbol{v}$ were initialized by randomly sampling from the uniform distribution on the interval $(-0.005, 0.005)$.

The final layer was created as a 3-layer MLP with 2000 hidden units each, and with ReLU activations.

Additionally, we used the Rmsprop optimizer with a learning rate of 0.001. We applied dropout of 0.25 only between the MLP layers of the Dense Layer.

Further, we found out that normalizing the capitalization of words by making all characters lowercase, and transforming numbers into a specific numeric token improved the model's performance while reducing the size of the embedding matrix. We also ignored the sentence pairs with a premise longer than 200 words during training (for improved memory stability), and those without a valid label ("-") both during training and validation.

Since one of the most conceptually important parts of our model was the raw sentence representation created in the Pooling Layer, we used four different methods for generating it (eqs. 4 – 7). Results are reported in Table 1.

We also tried using other architectures that rely on some sort of "inner" attention such as the *self-attentive* model proposed by Lin et al. (2017) and the *co-attentive* model by Xiong et al. (2016), but our preliminary results were not promising so we did not invest in fine-tuning them.

All the experiments were repeated without using character-level embeddings (i.e., $\boldsymbol{h}_i \in \mathbb{R}^{600}$).

4 Results

Table 1 presents the results of using different pooling strategies for generating a raw sentence representation vector from the word vectors. We can observe that that both the *mean* method, and picking the last hidden state for both directions performed slightly better than the two other strategies, however at 95% confidence we cannot assert that any of these methods is statistically different from one another.

This could be interpreted as if any of the four methods was good enough for capturing the overall meaning of the sentence, and the heavy lifting was done by the attention mechanism. It would be interesting to test these four strategies without the presence of attention to see whether it really plays an important role in this task or whether the predictive power lies within the sentence matching mechanism.

Method	w/o. chars	w. chars
mean	71.3 ± 1.2	71.3 ± 0.7
sum	70.7 ± 1.0	70.9 ± 0.8
last	70.9 ± 0.6	71.0 ± 1.2
max	70.6 ± 1.1	71.0 ± 1.1

Table 1: Mean matched validation accuracies (%) broken down by type of pooling method and presence or absence of character embeddings. Confidence intervals are calculated at 95% confidence over 10 runs for each method.

Another interesting result, as shown by Table 1 and Table 2, is that the model seemed to be insensitive to the usage of character embeddings, which was surprising because in our experiments with more complex models relying on shared information between premise and hypothesis, such as the one presented by Wang et al. (2017), the usage of character embeddings had a considerable impact

Method	w/o. chars	w. chars
mean	**72.3**	71.8
sum	71.6	71.6
last	71.4	**72.1**
max	71.1	71.6

Table 2: Best matched validation accuracies (%) obtained by each pooling method in presence and absence of character embeddings.

in model performance[2].

In Table 3 we report the accuracies obtained by our best model in both matched (first 5 genres) and mismatched (last 5 genres) development sets. We can observe that our implementation performed like ESIM overall, however ESIM relies on an attention mechanism that has access to both premise and hypothesis (Chen et al., 2017), while our model's treats each one separately. This supports the notion that inner attention is a powerful concept.

Genre	CBOW	ESIM	InnerAtt
Fiction	67.5	73.0	73.2
Government	67.5	74.8	75.2
Slate	60.6	67.9	67.2
Telephone	63.7	72.2	73.0
Travel	64.6	73.7	72.8
9/11	63.2	71.9	70.5
Face-to-face	66.3	71.2	74.5
Letters	68.3	74.7	75.4
Oup	62.8	71.7	71.5
Verbatim	62.7	71.9	69.5
MultiNLI Overall	**64.7**	**72.2**	**72.3**

Table 3: Validation accuracies (%) for our best model broken down by genre. Both CBOW and ESIM results are reported as in (Williams et al., 2017).

We picked the best model based on the best validation accuracy score obtained on the matched development set (72.257%). This model is as described in the previous section but without using character embeddings[3].

In addition, we created an ensemble by training 4 models as described earlier but initialized with different random seeds. The prediction is made by averaging the probability distributions returned by each model and then picking the class with the highest probability for each example. This improved our best test results, as reported by Kaggle, from 72.057% to 72.247% in the matched evaluation track, and from 72.055% to 72.827% in the mismatched evaluation track.

5 Conclusions and Future work

We presented the model used by the team Rivercorners in the 2017 RepEval shared task. Despite being conceptually simple and not relying on shared information between premise and hypothesis for encoding each sentence, nor on tree structures, our implementation achieved results as good as the ESIM model.

As future work we plan to incorporate part-of-speech embeddings to our implementation and concatenate them at the same level as we did with the character embeddings. We also plan to use pre-trained character embeddings to see whether they have any positive impact on performance.

Additionally, we think we could obtain better results by fine-tuning some hyperparameters such as the character embedding dimensions, the character-level LSTM encoder output dimension, and the Dense Layer architecture.

Further, we would like to see how different types of attention affect the overall performance. For this implementation we used the *concat* scoring scheme (eq. 8), as described by Luong et al. (2015), but there are several others that could provide better results.

Finally, we would like to exploit the structured nature of dependency parse trees by means of recursive neural networks (Tai et al., 2015) to enrich our initial sentence representations.

6 Resources

The code for replicating the results presented in this paper is available in the following link: `https://github.com/jabalazs/repeval_rivercorners`.

7 Acknowledgements

We thank the anonymous reviewers for helping us improve this paper through their feedback.

[2]This type of models were not allowed in this competition which is why we do not report further on them.

[3]Without the use of character embeddings, the sentence representations are 600-dimensional.

References

Samuel R. Bowman, Gabor Angeli, Christopher Potts, and Christopher D. Manning. 2015. A large annotated corpus for learning natural language inference. In *Proceedings of the 2015 Conference on Empirical Methods in Natural Language Processing*. Association for Computational Linguistics, Lisbon, Portugal, pages 632–642. http://aclweb.org/anthology/D15-1075.

Qian Chen, Xiaodan Zhu, Zhen-Hua Ling, Si Wei, Hui Jiang, and Diana Inkpen. 2017. Enhanced lstm for natural language inference. In *Proc. ACL*.

Sepp Hochreiter and Jürgen Schmidhuber. 1997. Long short-term memory. *Neural Computation* 9(8):1735–1780. http://www.bioinf.jku.at/publications/older/2604.pdf.

Jerrold J. Katz. 1972. *Semantic Theory*. Harper & Row, New York.

Zhouhan Lin, Minwei Feng, Cicero Nogueira dos Santos, Mo Yu, Bing Xiang, Bowen Zhou, and Yoshua Bengio. 2017. A structured self-attentive sentence embedding. In *Proceedings of the 5th International Conference on Learning Representations (ICLR)*. https://arxiv.org/pdf/1703.03130.pdf.

Yang Liu, Chengjie Sun, Lei Lin, and Xiaolong Wang. 2016. Learning natural language inference using bidirectional LSTM model and inner-attention. *CoRR* abs/1605.09090. http://arxiv.org/pdf/1605.09090.pdf.

Thang Luong, Hieu Pham, and Christopher D. Manning. 2015. Effective Approaches to Attention-based Neural Machine Translation. In *Proceedings of the 2015 Conference on Empirical Methods in Natural Language Processing*. Association for Computational Linguistics, Lisbon, Portugal, pages 1412–1421. http://aclweb.org/anthology/D15-1166.

Lili Mou, Hao Peng, Ge Li, Yan Xu, Lu Zhang, and Zhi Jin. 2015. Discriminative neural sentence modeling by tree-based convolution. In *Proceedings of the 2015 Conference on Empirical Methods in Natural Language Processing*. Association for Computational Linguistics, Lisbon, Portugal, pages 2315–2325. http://aclweb.org/anthology/D15-1279.

Jeffrey Pennington, Richard Socher, and Christopher D. Manning. 2014. Glove: Global vectors for word representation. In *Empirical Methods in Natural Language Processing (EMNLP)*. pages 1532–1543. http://www.aclweb.org/anthology/D14-1162.

Kai Sheng Tai, Richard Socher, and Christopher D. Manning. 2015. Improved semantic representations from tree-structured long short-term memory networks. *arXiv preprint arXiv:1503.00075* https://arxiv.org/pdf/1503.00075.pdf.

Johan van Benthem. 2008. A brief history of natural logic. In M. Chakraborty, B. Löwe, M. Nath Mitra, and S. Sarukki, editors, *Logic, Navya-Nyaya and Applications: Homage to Bimal Matilal*, College Publications.

Oriol Vinyals, Lukasz Kaiser, Terry Koo, Slav Petrov, Ilya Sutskever, and Geoffrey Hinton. 2015. Grammar as a foreign language. In *Advances in Neural Information Processing Systems*. pages 2773–2781. http://papers.nips.cc/paper/5635-grammar-as-a-foreign-language.

Zhiguo Wang, Wael Hamza, and Radu Florian. 2017. Bilateral multi-perspective matching for natural language sentences. *CoRR* abs/1702.03814. http://arxiv.org/abs/1702.03814.

Adina Williams, Nikita Nangia, and Samuel R. Bowman. 2017. A broad-coverage challenge corpus for sentence understanding through inference http://arxiv.org/pdf/1704.05426.pdf.

Caiming Xiong, Victor Zhong, and Richard Socher. 2016. Dynamic coattention networks for question answering. *arXiv preprint arXiv:1611.01604* .

LCT-MALTA's Submission to RepEval 2017 Shared Task

Hoa Trong Vu, Thuong-Hai Pham, Xiaoyu Bai
Marc Tanti, Lonneke van der Plas, Albert Gatt
thuong-hai.pham.16@um.edu.mt, hoa.vutrong.16@um.edu.mt, xiaoyu.bai.16@um.edu.mt
marctanti@gmail.com, lonneke.vanderplas@um.edu.mt, albert.gatt@um.edu.mt
Institute of Linguistics, University of Malta, Malta

Abstract

We present in this paper our team LCT-MALTA's submission to the RepEval 2017 Shared Task on natural language inference. Our system is a simple system based on a standard BiLSTM architecture, using as input GloVe word embeddings augmented with further linguistic information. We use max pooling on the BiLSTM outputs to obtain embeddings for sentences. On both the matched and the mismatched test sets, our system clearly beats the shared task's BiLSTM baseline model.

1 Introduction

The RepEval 2017 Shared Task aims to evaluate fixed-length vector representations (or embeddings) of sentences on the basis of a natural language understanding task, viz. natural language inference (NLI), also known as recognising textual entailments. Given two sentences, the first being the premise and the second the hypothesis, the goal of NLI is to train a classifier to predict whether the relation of the hypothesis to the premise is one of entailment, contradiction or a neutral relation. The training and test data for this 3-way classification task at RepEval 2017 are drawn from the Multi-Genre NLI, or MultiNLI corpus (see Williams et al. (2017) for details). Task participants are provided with both training and development datasets, where parts of the development data match the training data in terms of genre, topic etc. (referred to as *matched* examples) and other parts do not (referred to as *mismatched* examples).

This paper presents Team LCT-MALTA's submission to the shared task. In line with previous research, we obtain a single vector which is the combined representation of both the premise and the hypothesis and feed it into a Multilayer Perceptron (MLP) for the actual 3-way classification.

2 Related Work

Various works in recent years have dealt with the creation of distributed sentence representations, typically based on existing word embeddings such as word2vec (Mikolov et al., 2013) or GloVe (Pennington et al., 2014). The baseline models at the shared task use GloVe vectors and present three approaches to obtaining sentence embeddings (Williams et al., 2017): a) taking the sum of the embeddings of all the words in the sentence (continous bag of words, CBOW); b) taking the average of the hidden state outputs of a bidirectional LSTM (BiLSTM; Hochreiter and Schmidhuber 1997) across all the words; and c) the Enhanced Sequential Inference Model (ESIM) by (Chen et al., 2017), which, however, relies on cross-sentence attention, which submissions to the shared task may not make use of.

Instead of the BiLSTM architecture, Tai et al. (2015) propose a tree-structured LSTM to capture the hierarchical structure of natural language sentences. Conneau et al. (2017) use BiLSTM with max pooling and achieve state-of-art results when testing their sentence representations on an NLI task based on the Stanford Natural Language Inference (SNLI) dataset (Bowman et al., 2015). Lin et al. (2017) introduce a self-attention mechanism with multiple hops of attention on top of BiLSTM, where the different hops attend to different parts of the input sentence. Their approach represents sentence embeddings as 2-D matrices instead of vectors.

Proceedings of the 2nd Workshop on Evaluating Vector-Space Representations for NLP, pages 56–60,
Copenhagen, Denmark, September 7–11, 2017. ©2017 Association for Computational Linguistics

3 Our Approach

We present in our submission a simple BiLSTM-based approach related to the second baseline model. Crucially, however, we add the following alterations:

- Our input word vectors are enhanced with part-of-speech (POS), dependency and word character information.
- Instead of taking the average of the BiLSTM outputs across all words (mean pooling), we use max pooling.

3.1 Enhanced Word Embeddings

A central component of our approach is the enhancement of the pre-trained GloVe vectors with additional linguistic information. The main motivation is the following: BiLSTM proceeds linearly, processing an input sentence word by word. The structure of natural language sentences, however, is hierarchical in nature [1]. We wish to encode some information on linguistic structure while keeping the simple, standard BiLSTM architecture. Therefore, we attach such additional information to the representations of individual words.

In conrete terms, we initialise our model with 300-D pre-trained GloVe vectors (as is done in the BiLSTM baseline model) and enhance them with the following content:

3.1.1 POS-tag Embeddings

Part-of-speech (POS) tagging is a common first step in syntactic sentence processing. We postulate that explicit knowledge of a the input words' syntactic categories might help representing the meaning of the input sentence. Thus, using modules from UDPipe (Straka et al., 2016), we tokenise and tag input sentences with universal POS-tags. We then generate randomly-initialised, 20-D embeddings for all POS-tags.

3.1.2 Dependency Label Embeddings

Dependency parsing captures the binary dependency relation between words in a sentence and determines the central word of an input sentence (the head word of the sentence) (Kübler et al., 2009). In particular, it is enable to encode longer dependencies across multiple words. As such, dependency parsing provides vital information on the sentence's structure.

Hence, we apply UDPipe's (Straka et al., 2016) state-of-the-art dependency parser to the input sentence and subsequently equip each pre-trained word embedding with that word's dependency information, which in turn consists of the word's head word and its dependency relation to the head. In concrete terms, for each word w_i, we map the embedding of its head word w_j to a 50-D vector and generate a 50-D randomly initialised embedding for the dependency relation from w_i to its head. We then take the element-wise product between these two 50-D vectors to obtain the full dependency embedding for the word w_i. Formally, the dependency embedding w_{i_d} for any token w_i is computed as follows:

$$w_{i_d} = E_d[d_{ij}] \odot (W_d * w_j) \tag{1}$$

where d_{ij} is the dependency relation between token w_i and the head token w_j, E_d is the 50-D embedding of that dependency relation, W_d is a matrix of size 50x300 which maps w_j (originally a 300-D GloVe vector) to a 50-D vector, and $\odot$ is the element-wise product.

3.1.3 Character Embeddings

The usage of character embeddings is mainly inspired by various works which incorporate character-level embeddings into the distributed representation of words to yield improved word embeddings (Santos and Zadrozny, 2014; Bojanowski et al., 2016; Kim et al., 2016). For each token, we employ LSTMs to compute embeddings for each of its characters. The LSTM input at each time step is one character, i.e. one letter, and the output is a 100-D hidden state. The last 100-D hidden state vector is then considered the full character embedding for that token.

3.1.4 Final Input Word Embeddings

Finally, for each word, we concatenate its original GloVe embeddings with all of the above-mentioned additional linguistic information. Thus, our final embedding for each word, which we input to the BiLSTM to compute sentence embeddings, consists of the concatenation of the word's 300-D Glove embedding, its 20-D POS-tag embedding, its 50-D dependency embedding and 100-D character embedding. As mentioned, all of the embeddings except for the GloVe

[1] As mentioned in section 2, Tai et al. (2015) propose a *tree*-structured LSTM for similar reasons

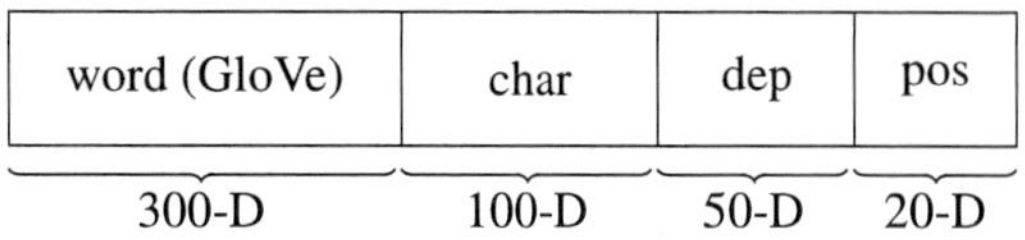

Figure 1: Our enhanced word embedding

word embeddings are randomly initialized. Figure 1 illustrates an instance of our final enhanced word embeddings.

3.2 BiLSTM Sentence Embedding with Max Pooling

The enhanced word embeddings described above are fed into a standard BiLSTM architecture, with a 100-D hidden state output vector for each unidirectional LSTM. Concatenating the forward ($\overrightarrow{h_t}$) and backward ($\overleftarrow{h_t}$) output vectors for each node, we obtain n hidden state vectors $\overrightarrow{h}$, where n is the number of words in the input sentence and $\overrightarrow{h}$ is a 200-D vector corresponding to one word.

$$\overrightarrow{h_t} = \overrightarrow{LSTM}(w_t, \overrightarrow{h_{t-1}}) \quad (2)$$

$$\overleftarrow{h_t} = \overleftarrow{LSTM}(w_t, \overleftarrow{h_{t-1}}) \quad (3)$$

Conneau et al. (2017) examine various supervised methods of obtaining general-purpose sentence embeddings, with their conclusion favouring a BiLSTM architecture combined with max pooling. We follow their findings and use max pooling on the n BiLSTM hidden outputs $\overrightarrow{h}$. Indeed, our own experiments shall show the superiority of max pooling over average pooling (see section 4). Hence, for each dimension d of the 200 dimensions, we take the maximum among the values of all hidden outputs at d. The result is a single 200-D vector embedding of the input sentence.

3.3 Combining Premise and Hypothesis Representations

We separately obtain the previously described sentence embeddings for the premise and the hypothesis. Mou et al. (2015) examine multiple heuristics for combining the same-length embeddings of two sentences in NLI tasks, including concatenating the two vectors and taking their element-wise difference or product. We use a combination of some of these heuristics. More specifically, we concatenate the two sentence embeddings, then further concatenate a) their element-wise maximum and b) their element-wise product to the concatenation of the two sentence embeddings. Hence, we obtain as a result a single 800-D vector that is the combined representation of the premise and the hypothesis.

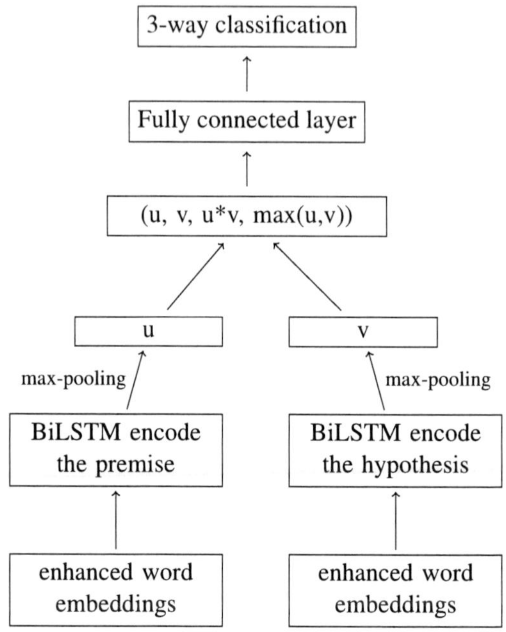

Figure 2: Architecture of our final submission

3.4 Classification

Finally, we feed the single vector representation of the two sentences to a *tanh* layer with a *softmax* layer on top of it to perform the 3-way classification to the classes *entailment*, *contradiction*, and *neutral*. Our complete model is illustrated in Figure 2.

4 Experiments & Results

We experimented with BiLSTM-based sentence encoders including and excluding our enhanced word embeddings as well as in combination with max pooling and average pooling. We use L2 regularization and set dropout rate to 0.1 to prevent overfitting. The models are trained in 10 epoches using Adam optimizer with learning rate 10^{-3}. The models having the best performance on development set are selected to evaluate on test set.

Furthermore, we implemented two systems presented in literature, viz. (Lin et al., 2017)'s self-attentive embeddings approach and (Kim, 2014)'s convolutional neural network (CNN) approach, and compared their performance with that of our

Method	Matched		Mismatched	
	Dev	Test	Dev	Test
BiLSTM + average pooling (baseline)	66.9	_	66.9	_
BiLSTM + max pooling	67.23	_	67.18	_
CNN (Kim, 2014)	67.3	_	68.0	_
Automatically learned self-attentive embeddings (Lin et al., 2017)	67.89	_	67.69	_
BiLSTM + enhanced embedding + average pooling	68.3	_	67.8	_
BiLSTM + enhanced embedding + max pooling	70.8	**70.7**	71.1	**70.8**

Table 1: System performances on MultiNLI dataset in order of ascending accuracy scores.

system. In their original work, Lin et al. (2017) use 30 hops of attention for each sentence. In our implementation of their algorithm, we deemed 10 hops to be sufficient due to the limited length of the sentences in our MultiNLI database.

The results of our experiments are shown in Table 1, in order of ascending accuracy scores. In our experiments, our final submission, i.e. the BiLSTM-encoder with enhanced word embeddings and max pooling, as described in section 3, performed best, obtaining accuracy scores of **70.8** and **71.1** on the matched and mismatched dev set, respectively. Its final results on the full shared task test set are **70.7** for matched and **70.8** for mismatched data.

5 Discussion

Our results favour max pooling over average pooling, which is in agreement with findings by Conneau et al. (2017). Moreover, our enhanced word embeddings are shown to be effective. Their addition alone produces the accuracy scores superior to what the incorporation of (Lin et al., 2017)'s automatically learned self-attention matrix yields. The combination of max pooling and enhanced word embeddings, which are extremely simple alterations to the BiLSTM baseline, yield results which clearly beat the baseline.

Thus, our submitted system to the RepEval 2017 shared task demonstrates that simple alterations to the standard BiLSTM architecture for computing sentence embeddings can obtain visible improvements. In particular, *linguistic* information is shown to be useful for the present NLI task. Therefore, with respect to distributed representations of sentence meaning, more sophisticated systems which take into account linguistic and grammatical relationships are worth further investigation.

References

Piotr Bojanowski, Edouard Grave, Armand Joulin, and Tomas Mikolov. 2016. Enriching word vectors with subword information. *arXiv preprint arXiv:1607.04606* .

Samuel R Bowman, Gabor Angeli, Christopher Potts, and Christopher D Manning. 2015. A large annotated corpus for learning natural language inference. *arXiv preprint arXiv:1508.05326* .

Qian Chen, Xiaodan Zhu, Zhen-Hua Ling, Si Wei, Hui Jiang, and Diana Inkpen. 2017. Enhanced lstm for natural language inference. In *Proc. ACL*.

Alexis Conneau, Douwe Kiela, Holger Schwenk, Loic Barrault, and Antoine Bordes. 2017. Supervised learning of universal sentence representations from natural language inference data. *arXiv preprint arXiv:1705.02364* .

Sepp Hochreiter and Jürgen Schmidhuber. 1997. Long short-term memory. *Neural computation* 9(8):1735–1780.

Yoon Kim. 2014. Convolutional neural networks for sentence classification. *arXiv preprint arXiv:1408.5882* .

Yoon Kim, Yacine Jernite, David Sontag, and Alexander M Rush. 2016. Character-aware neural language models. In *Thirtieth AAAI Conference on Artificial Intelligence*.

Sandra Kübler, Ryan McDonald, and Joakim Nivre. 2009. Dependency parsing. *Synthesis Lectures on Human Language Technologies* 1(1):1–127.

Zhouhan Lin, Minwei Feng, Cicero Nogueira dos Santos, Mo Yu, Bing Xiang, Bowen Zhou, and Yoshua Bengio. 2017. A structured self-attentive sentence embedding. *arXiv preprint arXiv:1703.03130* .

Tomas Mikolov, Ilya Sutskever, Kai Chen, Greg S Corrado, and Jeff Dean. 2013. Distributed representations of words and phrases and their compositionality. In *Advances in neural information processing systems*. pages 3111–3119.

Lili Mou, Rui Men, Ge Li, Yan Xu, Lu Zhang, Rui Yan, and Zhi Jin. 2015. Natural language inference by tree-based convolution and heuristic matching. *arXiv preprint arXiv:1512.08422* .

Jeffrey Pennington, Richard Socher, and Christopher D Manning. 2014. Glove: Global vectors for word representation. In *EMNLP*. volume 14, pages 1532–1543.

Cicero D Santos and Bianca Zadrozny. 2014. Learning character-level representations for part-of-speech tagging. In *Proceedings of the 31st International Conference on Machine Learning (ICML-14)*. pages 1818–1826.

Milan Straka, Jan Hajic, and Jana Straková. 2016. Ud-pipe: Trainable pipeline for processing conll-u files performing tokenization, morphological analysis, pos tagging and parsing. In *Proceedings of the Tenth International Conference on Language Resources and Evaluation (LREC 2016)*.

Kai Sheng Tai, Richard Socher, and Christopher D Manning. 2015. Improved semantic representations from tree-structured long short-term memory networks. *arXiv preprint arXiv:1503.00075* .

Adina Williams, Nikita Nangia, and Samuel R Bowman. 2017. A broad-coverage challenge corpus for sentence understanding through inference. *arXiv preprint arXiv:1704.05426* .

Author Index

Association for Computational Linguistics
209 N. Eighth Street
Stroudsburg, Pennsylvania 18360

ISBN 978-1-5108-4750-7

9 781510 847507

CURRAN ASSOCIATES INC.
proceedings.com